All-American
CAKES,
PIES,
COOKIES
& TREATS

All-American
CAKES, PIES, COOKIES & TREATS
60 SIMPLE & TRADITIONAL SWEETS

Roy Fares

PHOTOGRAPHY **WOLFGANG KLEINSCHMIDT**

TRANSLATED BY CHRISTIAN GULLETTE

Skyhorse Publishing

CONTENTS

Introduction
SWEET AMERICA

» **Cookies, donuts,** cheesecakes, bundt cakes, fudge, pop tarts, cake pops, blondies, cupcakes. The list of American baked goods could go on and on. Ever since I began my training as a pastry chef, I've been interested in American sweets. The culture and desserts from these United States of cakes have, in fact, spread across the world.

I don't actually know why I came to like these baked goods so early on. Maybe it's because I have always been fascinated by the United States. The first time I traveled there, I immediately felt like I fit right in. Since then I've returned many times, mainly to Los Angeles, and I've lived there periodically. And my love for California has only grown. Why has California become my absolute favorite vacation destination? I don't actually know that either. One reason may be that I come from the Lebanese culture, with its touch of crazy social chaos (cheek kisses, loud conversation, people in touch with their emotions). I feel that this way of life definitely fits California. Another reason is that there is a really permissive attitude there, for the most part. It is okay to be who you are, to be different, and to believe in yourself.

At first, I thought that the majority of American baked goods I tasted had a little too much sugar and too much of everything on the outside, but at the same time I fell totally in love with *double chocolate, triple fudge*—it's like double and triple everything! At least! And who doesn't love that?

You could say that this book originates from a pure curiosity of American baking culture. After spending a lot of time in California, I feel that I probably have enough knowledge and contacts to present my favorite recipes. The United States of America is huge, and there is, of course, a never-ending amount of baked goods to discover in this country, but in this book I've picked just over fifty recipes that I think are the best of all. The recipes are American at their core, but I have adapted them a bit according to my own palette. That is to say, I've concentrated the flavors and reduced the amount of sugar a little.

If the recipe doesn't specify chilled ingredients, then room temperature ingredients generally give the best results. Oven temperatures in the book are specifically for convection ovens. If you are baking with a regular oven, then you ought to raise the temperature about 25 degrees Fahrenheit (4 degrees Celsius). If you live at a higher altitude, you'll have to adjust accordingly to compensate for the atmospheric pressure. And definitely use the weights specified in the recipes—that will give you more precise results. Good luck!

Soft
CAKES

PAL

M SPRINGS

>> Between Los Angeles and San Diego in a valley in Riverside County lies the little desert city of **Palm Springs**. Here you'll notice that you're in the Colorado Desert because it is warm—year round and twenty-four hours a day. During the summer, it is not unusual for temperatures to reach over 100 degrees Fahrenheit (40 degrees Celsius) during the day and just over 70 degrees Fahrenheit (20 degrees Celsius) at night. But it is during the winter that Palm Springs is most popular, when the weather is roughly like a nice, Swedish summer day. That is to say, 70-75 degrees Fahrenheit (20-25 degrees Celsius).

Palm Springs is called "Hollywood's playground" because movie stars have been coming here to relax for almost a hundred years. The city is barely two hours by car from Hollywood. Here, there is a Walk of Stars, with sidewalks honoring stars such as Elvis Presley, Sophia Loren, Liberace, and Ginger Rogers.

I absolutely love Palm Springs! The whole city is like one big resort. A well-maintained, neat, idyllic small town with a mixture of people from all kinds of different social, economical, and racial backgrounds. I come here to enjoy lazy days by the pool. And speaking of water—all plants, lawns, and palms are totally dependent on intensive irrigation, for here in the desert it rarely rains. But the climate is ideal for growing dates, and during a visit to such a farm, I got the inspiration for the date cake on page 17. It can be fairly windy, and to make the most of the energy, huge wind farms have been erected along the highway. It feels so awesome to rush past row after row of these spinning giants. The city center is really just one long street with shops, typical of smaller American cities.

BANANA NUT BREAD

A moist and long-lasting cake with the advantage that it's baked with slightly overripe bananas. The taste is deeper and better that way. Sometimes I toast the slices and spread Nutella or peanut butter on them. Yum!

16 Slices

2 cups (240 g) all-purpose flour
1 tsp (5 g) baking soda
½ tsp (3 g) salt
4 (550 g) bananas
½ cup (60 g) walnuts
½ cup + 1 tsp (120 g) room temperature salted butter
½ cup + 1 tbsp (110 g) brown sugar
2 (110 g) eggs

Set the oven to 350 degrees Fahrenheit (170 degrees Celsius), convection function. Butter an oblong baking form, ½ quart (1½ liters). Lightly flour the form's sides and cover the bottom with parchment paper.

Sift the flour, baking soda, and salt into a bowl. Mash the bananas and chop the nuts. In another bowl, whip together the butter and brown sugar until fluffy. Whip one egg at a time into the butter mixture. Add the mashed bananas and the dry ingredients along with the walnuts. Stir together into a smooth batter.

Distribute the batter evenly in the pan and bake in the middle of the oven for 40–45 minutes. Test the cake with a toothpick to be sure it is baked through.

Let the cake stand in the pan for 10 minutes. Turn over onto a rack and allow to cool.

SPICY DATE LOAF

Dates have been growing in the United States since the early 1900s. One of the largest growers is Shields, where I went for a visit. The farm is located just outside Palm Springs in the Coachella Valley. The warm and dry climate is perfect for date trees. To be completely honest, I wasn't a big fan of dates before. But when I tasted a sugary-sweet date just melt in my mouth, I was totally converted. Now I love dates!

Preheat the oven to 350 degrees Fahrenheit (170 degrees Celsius), convection function. Grease an oblong baking pan, 8 cup (2 liters). Lightly flour the edges of the pan and line the base with baking paper.

Chop the dates and let them soak in ¾ cup (190 mL) of orange juice for 30 minutes. Stir occasionally. Chop the pecans.

In a bowl, whisk together the butter, brown sugar, and the vanilla extract with an electric mixer until fluffy, scraping the sides with a spatula in between. Then add the eggs one at a time, continuing to whisk until it becomes a smooth mixture. In a bowl, sift the dry ingredients and stir them together with 1 ¼ cup (285 mL) of orange juice and zest in batches. Stir until it becomes a smooth paste. Add in the nuts along with the dates and the orange juice they've been soaking in. Divide the batter evenly in the pan.

Bake in the oven for about 60 minutes. Use a toothpick to be sure that it is baked through. Let the cake stand in the mold for 10 minutes, then turn out onto a rack and allow to cool.

20 slices

2 cups (300 g) pitted dates
¾ cup (200 mL (200 g)) freshly-squeezed orange juice
1⅓ cups (150 g) pecans
½ cup (120 g) room temperature unsalted butter
1 cup (170 g) brown sugar
2 (110 g) eggs
½ tbsp (5 g) vanilla extract
3⅓ cups (480 g) all-purpose flour
1 tbsp (15 g) baking powder
¾ tsp (8 g) baking soda
2 tsp (5 g) ground cinnamon
2 tsp (4 g) ground nutmeg
1 tsp (2 g) ground cloves
1 tsp (7 g) salt
1¼ cups (300 mL (300 g)) freshly-squeezed orange juice
Grated zest of 2 oranges

CARROT CAKE

This cake is moist, delicious and easy to make—a safe bet, simply put. And as some would say: it's also a little nutritious because it's made with carrots!

CARROT CAKE

Preheat the oven to 350 degrees Fahrenheit (180 degrees Celsius), convection function. Grease a pan, 13 × 9 inches (33 cm x 23 cm). Lightly flour the pan's edges and line the base with baking paper.

Sift the flour, baking soda, baking powder, salt, and cinnamon in a bowl and add the coconut. Whisk eggs and sugar with an electric mixer until white and fluffy in another bowl. Mix the oil and dry ingredients in batches into the egg mixture. Finally, stir in the carrots.

Spread the batter evenly in the pan and bake in the middle of the oven for about 25 minutes. Use a toothpick to be sure the cake is baked through. Allow to cool completely.

FROSTING

With an electric mixer, beat the butter and cream cheese until fluffy in a bowl. Add the powdered sugar and vanilla extract and whisk into a nice and firm frosting. Spread the frosting over the cake.

18–20 slices

CARROT CAKE
½ cup (35 g) shredded coconut
2 cups (270 g) all-purpose flour
1 tsp (5 g) baking soda
1½ tsp (7 g) baking powder
½ tsp (3 g) salt
2 tsp (4 g) ground cinnamon
4 (220 g) eggs
1⅓ cups (300 g) sugar
1⅓ (cups) (300 mL (260 g)) vegetable oil
About 6 (340 g) finely shredded carrots

FROSTING
¼ cup (50 g) room temperature unsalted butter
1⅓ cups (300 g) cream cheese
2¾ cups (330 g) powdered-sugar
1 tsp (3 g) vanilla extract

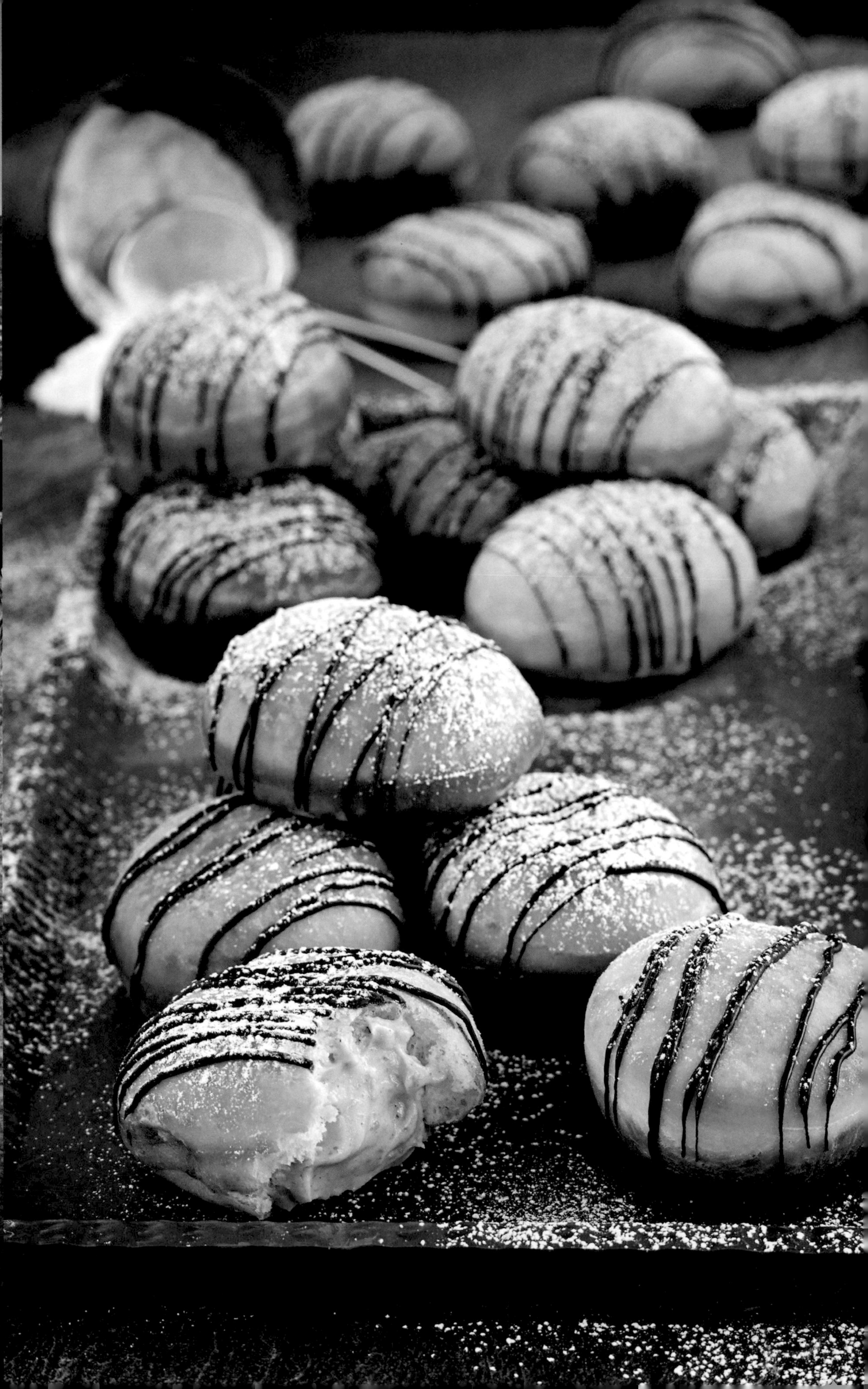

PEANUT BUTTER DONUTS

These donuts don't really fit into this chapter. But they're so good that I crammed them into the book anyway.

DOUGH

Warm the milk to 99 degrees Fahrenheit (37 degrees Celsius). Dissolve the yeast with the milk in a stand mixer. Add sugar, salt, eggs, egg yolk, butter, and three quarters of the flour (4 cups (525 g)). Knead the dough for 5 minutes on low speed, then add the remaining flour and knead the dough on medium speed until it begins to pull away from the edges.

Turn out the dough onto a floured baking sheet, cover with a kitchen towel and let rest for 20 minutes. Move the dough to a floured work surface and gently roll it out into a disk, approximately one half inch (1½ cm) thick. Use a cutter, 2½–3 inches (7–8 cm) in diameter, and cut out 25–30 circles and put them on plates with floured parchment paper. Cover with a kitchen towel and let rise until they've doubled in size, about 1½ hours.

Heat oil to 350 degrees Fahrenheit (180 degrees Celsius) in a pan with high edges. Fry the donuts for about 30 seconds on each side or until golden. Remove with a slotted spoon and let drain on paper towels. Allow to cool completely.

PEANUT FILLING

Stir together the cream cheese and peanut butter. Add the powdered sugar and whisk together with an electric mixer to form a fluffy mixture. Whip the cream until thick and then mix it into the peanut batter little by little. Fill a piping bag with the mixture, and insert a long, thin star-shaped piping tip into each donut and pipe in the filling.

GARNISH

Chop the chocolate and melt it gently in a water bath or in the microwave. Drizzle chocolate over each donut and finish by sprinkling a little powdered sugar.

25–30 donuts

DOUGH
1¼ cups (350 mL (350 g)) whole milk
1 tbsp (15 g) yeast
½ cup + 1 tbsp (100 g) sugar
1 tsp (6 g) salt
2 (110 g) eggs
1 (15 g) egg yolk
⅓ cup (70 g) room temperature unsalted butter
5¼ cups (750 g) all-purpose flour

4¼ cups (1 liter) vegetable oil for frying

PEANUT BUTTER FILLING
1¼ cups (300 g) cream cheese
½ cup (130 g) smooth peanut butter
1¼ cups (180 g) powdered sugar
¼ cup (50 mL (50 g)) whipping cream

GARNISH
⅓ cup (50–100 g) dark chocolate
Powdered sugar for dusting

APPLE CARDAMOM CAKE

The perfect cake for cozy, autumn days. Wonderfully powerful and with the full flavor of apple and cardamom. Serve as is, but a little vanilla whipped cream or vanilla ice cream, of course, is never wrong.

APPLE FILLING

Peel, core, and dice the apples into ¼ inch (½ cm) cubes. Put the pieces in a bowl with cinnamon and sugar. Mix and set aside.

CAKE

Preheat the oven to 350 degrees Fahrenheit (170 degrees Celsius), convection function. Grease and flour a round ring cake mold that holds at least 6 cups thoroughly. Sift the flour, baking powder, salt, and cardamom in a bowl. In another bowl, beat the butter for 3 minutes, add the sugar and vanilla extract, and with an electric mixer, whisk until it becomes a fluffy mixture. Add 1 egg at a time and mix well. Mix the dry ingredients with a bit of milk at a time and mix to a smooth batter.

Fill one quarter of the mold with batter and then sprinkle some apple bits. Continue alternating batter and filling. Bake in the center of the oven for 55–60 minutes. Use a toothpick to test that the cake is baked through. Let cake stand in the mold for 10 minutes. Turn the cake out onto a rack and let cool completely. Dust with powdered sugar.

18 slices

APPLE FILLING
2 large Granny Smith apples
2 tsp (4 g) ground cinnamon
2 tbsp (25 g) sugar

CAKE
3¼ cups (450 g) all-purpose flour
3 tsp (15 g) baking powder
½ tsp (3 g) salt
3 tsp (7 g) ground cardamom
1 cup + 2 tbsp (250 g) room temperature salted butter
1¾ cups (380 g) sugar
4 (240 g) eggs, room temperature
½ tbsp (5 g) vanilla extract
1 cup (237 mL (250 g)) whole milk
Powdered sugar for dusting

CHOCOLATE ESPRESSO BUNDT CAKE

Soft cakes almost always have icing on top. More is more! And I can only agree. This typical chocolate cake is the obvious choice for all chocolate and coffee lovers.

CHOCOLATE CAKE

Preheat the oven to 350 degrees Fahrenheit (175 degrees Celsius), convection function. Lightly butter and flour carefully a circular ring cake mold, 9 inches (23 cm) in diameter and at least 4 inches (10 cm) deep.

Sift the flour, baking powder, and salt in a bowl. Melt the butter in a saucepan, add the cocoa powder, espresso, and water and whisk into a smooth mixture. Remove the pan from the heat, add the sugar, sour cream, and eggs and mix well.

Mix in the dry ingredients and whisk together to a smooth paste. Pour the batter into the mold and bake in middle of the oven for about 45 minutes. Use a toothpick to test that the cake is baked-through. Let the cake stand in the mold for 10 minutes, then turn out onto a rack and let it cool completely.

CHOCOLATE GLAZE

Melt the butter, corn syrup or honey, and chocolate in a water bath. Stir together into a smooth icing. Let the icing cool to a lukewarm temperature. Place a baking sheet under the rack with the cooled cake, and pour the glaze over the cake. When the icing has solidified the cake can be transferred to a platter.

15 slices

CHOCOLATE CAKE

1⅔ cups (240 g) all-purpose flour
1 tsp (5 g) baking powder
¼ tsp (2 g) salt
1 cup (230 g) salted butter
⅔ cup (60 g) cocoa powder
1 shot of espresso
⅔ cup (157 mL (150 g)) water
2 cups (400 g) sugar
½ tbsp (5 g) vanilla extract
1 cup (250 g) sour cream
2 (110 g) eggs

CHOCOLATE GLAZE

⅓ cup (75 g) unsalted butter
1 tsp (8 g) corn syrup or honey
¾ cup (100 g) dark chocolate, 70%

FUDGE BROWNIES WITH FLAKED SALT

Classic brownies covered in a wonderful, chocolate-packed truffle icing topped with a little finely flaked salt. They can be baked a day in advance and refrigerated in an air-tight container.

TRUFFLE

Chop the chocolate and place in a bowl. In a small saucepan, bring the cream to a boil, pour it over the chocolate and let stand for a few minutes until chocolate has melted. Stir to a smooth ganache. Cover with plastic wrap and let stand at room temperature.

BROWNIE

Preheat the oven to 325 degrees Fahrenheit (160 degrees Celsius), convection function. Grease the edges of a baking pan, 8 × 8 inches (20 cm x 20 cm), and line the base with parchment paper.

Melt the butter over low heat in a saucepan. Add sugar, cacoa, salt, and vanilla extract and mix. (It may look a little grainy, but the flour will make the batter come together and become smooth and fine.) Gently whisk in one egg at a time, or work them with a spatula. Finally, fold in the flour and mix to a smooth paste.

Spread the batter evenly in the pan and bake in the middle of the oven for about 22 minutes. Allow to cool completely.

Remove the cake from the mold and remove the parchment paper. Turn the cake upside down and spread the truffle on top. If the truffle is too loose, set in the fridge for a while and it will thicken slightly. Sprinkle with sea salt and then let the cake stand in the fridge for about 40-50 minutes, so that the truffle hardens properly. Cut the cake into pieces and serve at room temperature.

16 pieces

TRUFFLE
1¼ cups (150 g) dark chocolate, 55%
⅔ cup (118 mL (150 g)) whipping cream
Flaked salt for sprinkling

BROWNIE
⅔ cup (150 g) unsalted butter
1 cup (250 g) sugar
⅔ cup (70 g) cocoa powder
½ tsp (3 g) salt
½ tsp (1½ g) vanilla extract
2 (110 g) eggs
½ cup (60 g) all-purpose flour

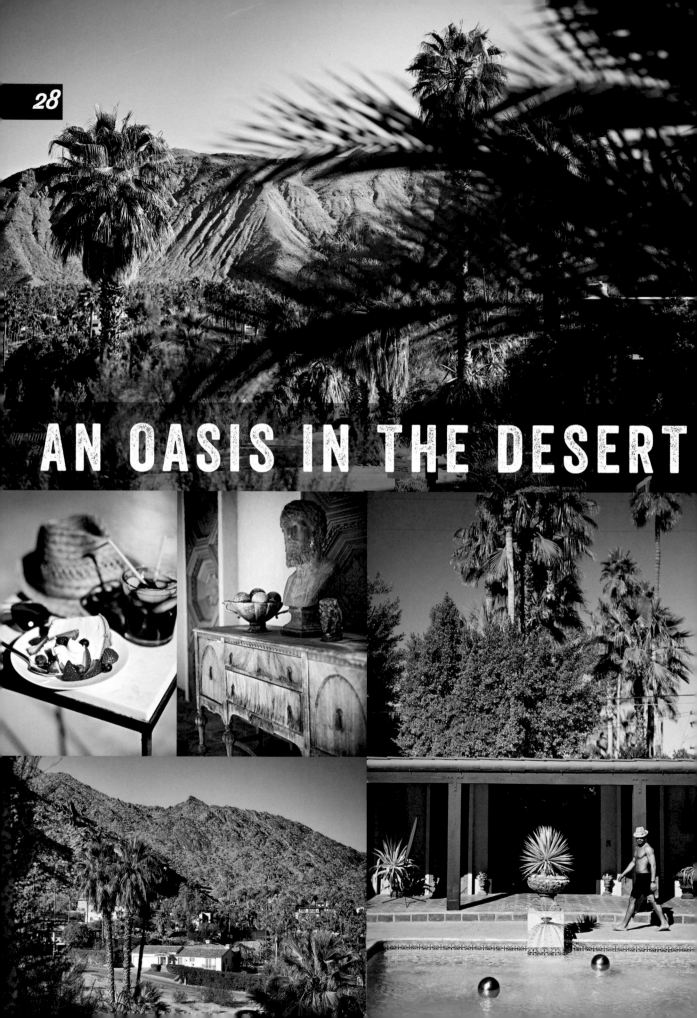

AN OASIS IN THE DESERT

In Palm Springs you can walk in the footsteps of the stars. Like Villa Carmelita, for example. My friend Rudi Polak currently owns this fantastic house that has served as a hideaway and playground for several Hollywood stars. In the villa, stars such as Kirk Douglas, Lloyd Bridges, and Sonny and Cher lounged, partied, and swam. It felt awesome to be there—and, of course, I couldn't help but celebrate the occasion with a little lemon and vanilla bundt cake (see page 30). Cakes are common at the cafes in Palm Springs. They keep so well in the warm climate.

LEMON AND VANILLA BUNDT CAKE

Fresh, summer lemon cake with a soft and sweet icing. Cake is often served with something on the side, as it is here with fresh berries and lightly-whipped cream.

LEMON CAKE

Preheat the oven to 325 degrees Fahrenheit (165 degrees Celsius), convection function. Grease and flour thoroughly a round ring cake mold, 9½ inches (24 cm) in diameter and at least 3 inches (8 cm) deep. Sift the flour, baking powder, and baking soda in a bowl. Using an electric mixer, beat the butter and sugar until fluffy in another bowl. Beat in the eggs one at a time into the butter mixture and then the dry ingredients in batches. Add the lemon juice and zest and stir together to a smooth batter.

Pour batter into the pan and bake in the oven for approximately 45 minutes. Use a toothpick to test that the cake is baked through. Let the cake stand in the mold for 20 minutes. Turn it out onto a rack and let cool completely.

VANILLA GLAZE

Heat the milk and butter in a saucepan over low heat until the butter has melted. Add the powdered sugar and vanilla extract and whisk until it becomes a rich glaze. Place baking paper under the rack with the cooled cake, pour the glaze around the middle of the cake and let it flow down nicely on the paper. When the glaze has set, the cake can be transferred to a platter.

15 slices

LEMON CAKE

1⅔ cups (240 g) all-purpose flour
¼ tsp (2 g) baking powder
¼ tsp (2 g) baking soda
1 cup (230 g) room temperature salted butter
2 cups (400 g) sugar
5 (275 g) eggs, room temperature
2 lemons, the juice from 2 and the zest from 1

VANILLA GLAZE

⅓ cup (79 mL (25 g)) whole milk
1 tbsp + 1 tsp (20 g) salted butter
1¼ cups (180 g) powdered sugar
½ tsp (1½ g) vanilla extract

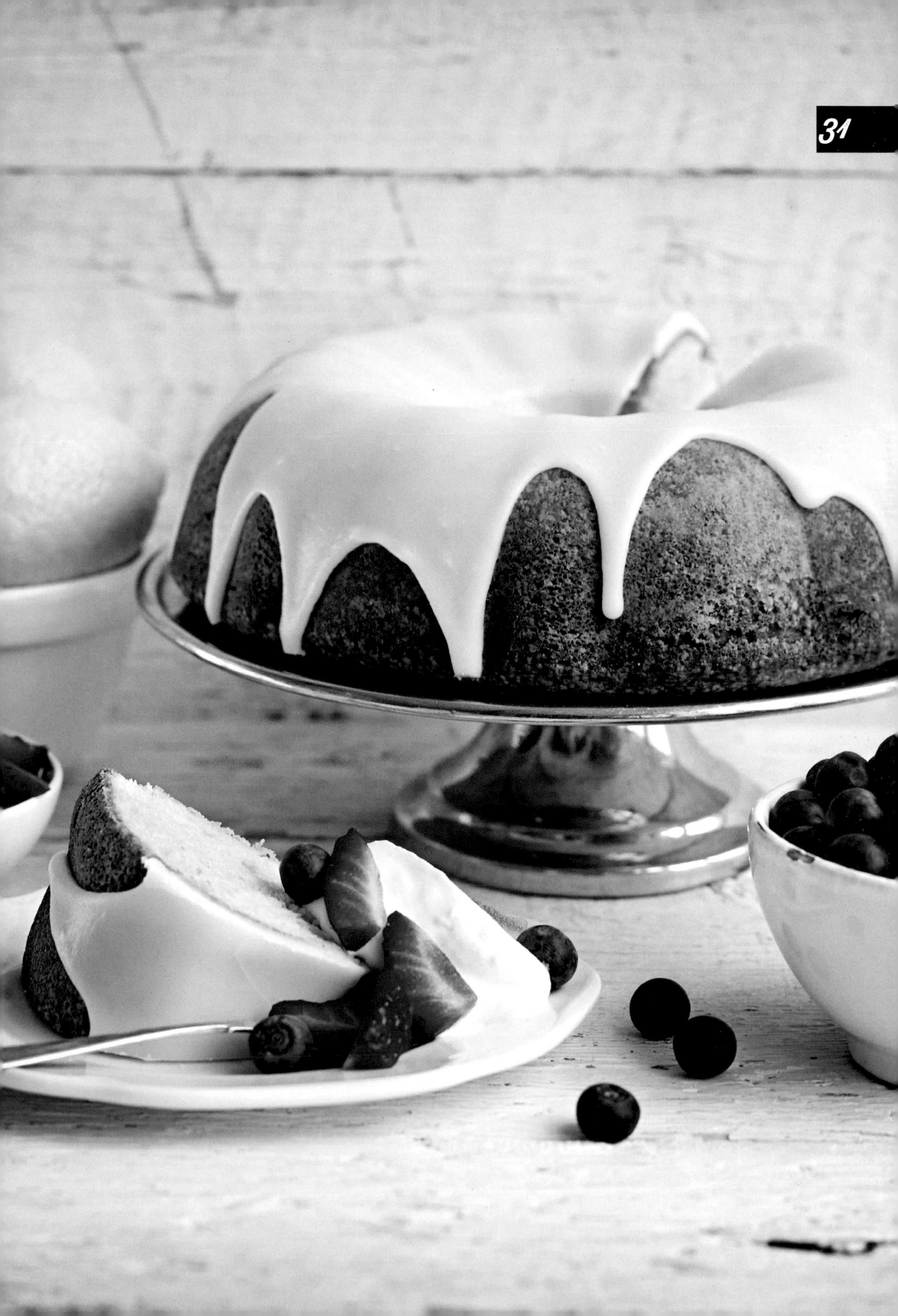

RASPBERRY BLONDIES

Blondies are like brownies, but with white chocolate. They're a bit sweeter, but with the slightly tart berries there's a nice balance. I am very fond of white chocolate, so this pastry is right in line with my tastes. They can be prepared in advance and stored cold. Serve them at room temperature.

Approx. 24 pieces

1¾ cups (330 g) solid white chocolate
¾ cup (160 g) salted butter
1½ cups (220 g) all-purpose flour
1 tsp (7 g) salt
½ tbsp (5 g) vanilla extract
3 (165 g) eggs, room temperature
½ cup (90 g) sugar
½ cup (70 g) white chocolate chips or coarsely-chopped
    white chocolate
30 fresh raspberries

Preheat the oven to 325 degrees Fahrenheit (165 degrees Celsius), convection function. Grease the edges of a pan, 12 × 8 inches (30 x 21 cm), and line the base with parchment paper.

Chop the white chocolate and melt it with the butter gently in a water bath or in the microwave. Sift the flour and salt in a bowl. Beat the eggs with the vanilla extract until fluffy with an electric mixer in a separate bowl. Whisk in the sugar and stir it into the melted chocolate and butter mixture. Add the dry ingredients and mix thoroughly.

Spread the batter evenly in the mold, sprinkle with white chocolate chips and the raspberries and bake in the middle of the oven for about 25 minutes. The cake should only get some light color. Let cool completely and then cut into pieces.

COOKIES
and
SWEETS

VENICE BEA

>> When the city of Venice, with all its canals, was founded in 1900 in Santa Monica Bay, Los Angeles, the area was intended to be a smaller counterpart to Italy's Venice. **Venice Beach** is the city's long beach—known as a place for the creative and the artistic.

Many may recognize Venice Beach from the TV series Baywatch, but the beach is so much more than just swimming and lifeguards! The multitude of people and all the colors feel almost unreal, a bit like being in another world or a circus. And here you definitely find all types of people—roller skaters, hippies, body builders, street performers, acrobats, surfers—all of them sun bathing in their swim suits. You can also find artists lining the boardwalk with their works for sale.

If you want time to see as much as possible, it's a smart idea to rent a bike and bike along the Santa Monica Bay—if you have the energy to bike from Venice Beach to Malibu. It's a magical bike ride with mile after mile of absolutely gorgeous beaches. Take something to drink and something energy-rich and delicious such as a packed lunch. How about some of the different cookies that I offer in this chapter?

I really love this place! I simply do not get the same kick out of seeing so many different types of people hanging out, eating, drinking, dancing, singing, working out, playing basketball, skateboarding, biking, jogging, and walking all in the same place anywhere else. Anyone can be here, and everyone fits in.

SNICKERDOODLES

Despite its name, these cookies contain nothing even resembling Snickers. No, these are soft, chewy cookies with the fine taste of cinnamon.

20 cookies

1¼ cups (170 g) all-purpose flour
½ tsp (3 g) baking soda
½ cup (100 g) room temperature salted butter
⅔ cup (160 g) sugar
½ tsp (2½ g) vanilla extract
1 (55 g) egg, room temperature
1 tsp (5 mL (5 g)) white distilled vinegar

GARNISH
¼ cup (45 g) sugar
1 tsp (2 g) ground cinnamon

Preheat oven to 400 degrees Fahrenheit (200 degrees Celsius), convection function. Mix the flour and baking soda in a bowl. Beat the butter, vanilla extract, and sugar until fluffy in a separate bowl. Beat in the egg. Add the dry ingredients and the vinegar. Work into a smooth dough.

Mix the sugar and cinnamon for the garnish and pour the mixture onto a plate. Divide the dough into 20 equal sized pieces, roll the pieces into balls and roll each ball in the sugar mixture. Place the balls with room in between on a baking sheet lined with parchment paper and flatten them slightly.

Bake in the oven until the cookies have browned slightly, about 8 minutes. Let the cookies cool for a few minutes and move them gently with a spatula to a rack to cool completely. Keep in a dry place.

PEANUT BUTTER COOKIES

A very traditional cookie with the nutty crunch of peanuts. I can picture every grandmother, if only for their grandchildren's sake, having a cookie jar filled with these chewy and crisp little goodies. And the kids drinking cold milk, of course, with these cookies. Milk and cookies, plain and simple!

Preheat the oven to 375 degrees Fahrenheit (190 degrees Celsius), convection function. With an electric mixer, whisk the butter, vanilla extract, peanut butter, sugar, and brown sugar in a bowl until fluffy. Sift the flour, baking powder, baking soda, and salt in a separate bowl. Mix the eggs and milk into the butter mixture. Stir in the dry ingredients and work into a dough. Lastly, work in the peanuts.

Divide the dough into about 26 pieces, roll the pieces into equal sized balls, and place them sparsely on 2 baking trays lined with parchment paper. Flatten the balls slightly and press with a fork to make a grid pattern on each cookie.

Bake in center of the oven for about 10 minutes or until the cookies have a golden color. Let the cookies cool a bit and then move them over to a rack to cool completely. Keep in a dry place.

26 cookies

½ cup (120 g) room temperature salted butter
½ cup + 1 tsp (120 g) crunchy peanut butter
½ cup (130 g) sugar
⅓ cup (70 g) brown sugar
½ tsp (2 g) vanilla extract
1⅔ cups (240 g) all-purpose flour
½ tsp (3 g) baking powder
1 tsp (5 g) baking soda
¼ tsp (2 g) salt
1 (55 g) egg, room temperature
1 tbsp (15 g) milk
½ cup (70 g) salted peanuts

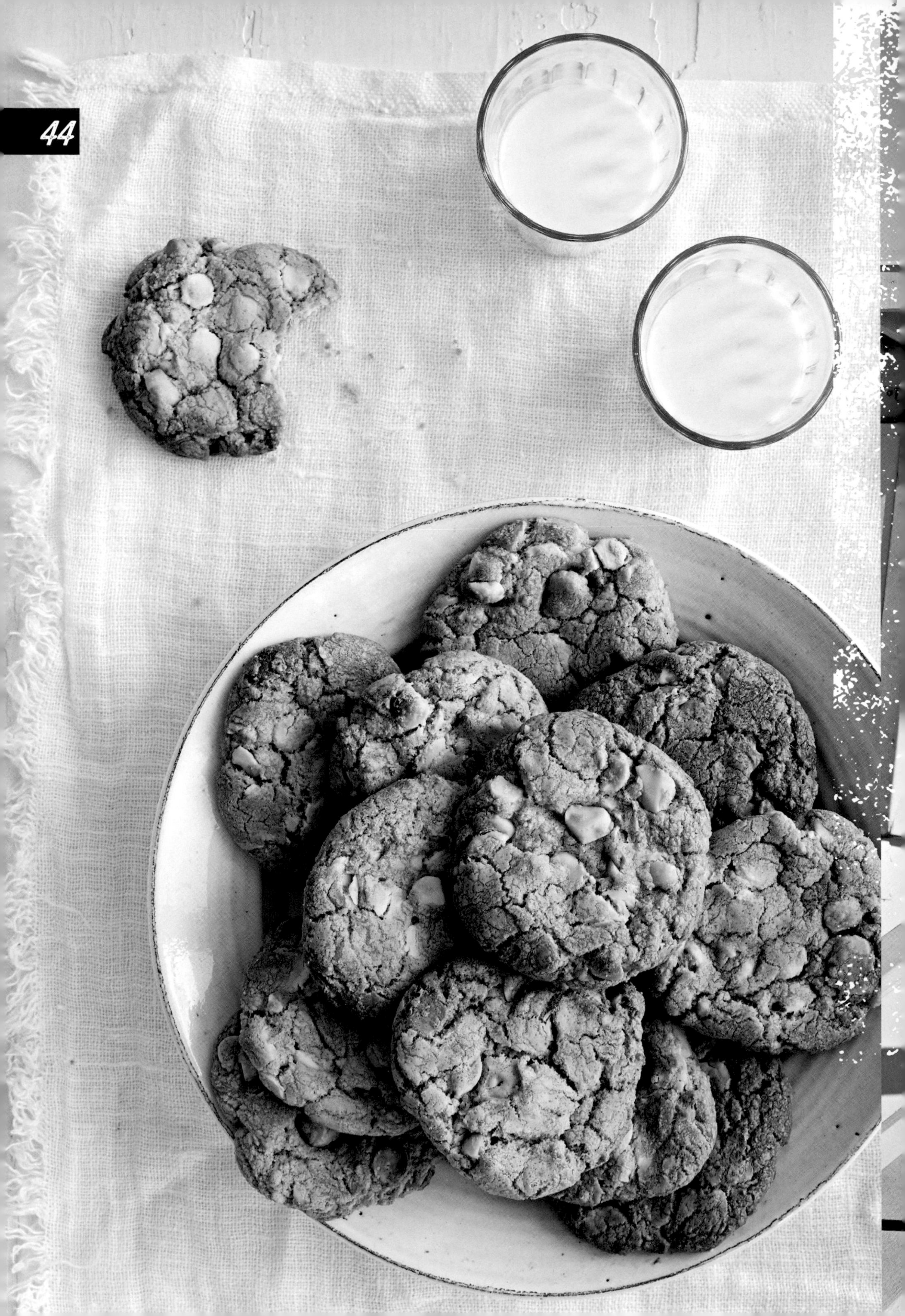

CHOCOLATE AND MACADAMIA NUT COOKIES

When I was in Hawaii, I fell in love with macadamia nuts. So I was, of course, delighted when I came across this cookie. Best of all, it contains white chocolate!

26 cookies

¾ cup (170 g) salted butter
1⅓ cups (180 g) macadamia nuts
¾ cup (140 g) brown sugar
⅔ cup (120 g) sugar
½ tsp (2 g) vanilla extract
2¼ cups (300 g) all-purpose flour
½ tsp (3 g) baking soda
¼ tsp (2 g) salt
1 (55 g) egg
1 (15 g) egg yolk
1½ cups (250 g) white chocolate chips or chopped white chocolate

Preheat the oven to 340 degrees Fahrenheit (170 degrees Celsius), convection function. Melt the butter and coarsely chop the nuts. Stir together the butter, vanilla extract, brown sugar, and sugar in a bowl. Sift the dry ingredients in a separate bowl. Beat the eggs and yolk into the butter mixture. Add the dry ingredients and work into a dough. Work in the nuts and chocolate chips. Wrap the dough and let it rest in the fridge for about 20 minutes.

   Divide the dough into 26 pieces, roll them into equal sized balls, and place them sparsely on 2 baking sheets lined with parchment paper. Flatten the balls slightly and bake them in the oven for about 11 minutes or until the cookies have a nice color. Let the cookies cool slightly and then finish cooling completely on cooling racks. Keep in a dry place.

CHOCOLATE CHIP COOKIES

This chewy and crispy cookie with a little, nutty crunch is the most traditional cookie you can bake. And once you've taken one, it's hard not to take another, and another. . .

30 cookies

¾ cup (130 g) hazelnuts
1¼ cups (300 g) dark chocolate or chocolate chips
1 cup (230 g) room temperature salted butter
¾ cup (170 g) sugar
⅔ cup (120 g) brown sugar
½ tsp (1½ g) vanilla extract
2⅔ cups (330 g) all-purpose flour
1½ tsp (7 g) baking soda
½ tsp (3 g) salt
1 (55 g) egg

Preheat the oven to 375 degrees Fahrenheit (190 degrees Celsius), convection function. Pour the hazelnuts into a pan and roast them in the oven for about 8 minutes. Let the nuts cool, put them in a clean kitchen hand towel, and scrub off the shells. Chop the hazelnuts and whole chocolate fairly coarsely (chocolate chips do not need to be chopped). With an electric mixer, beat the butter, vanilla extract, sugar, and brown sugar in a bowl until fluffy. Mix the dry ingredients in a separate bowl. Stir the egg into the butter mixture. Add the dry ingredients and work together to form a dough. Work in the chopped nuts and chocolate.

Divide the dough into 30 pieces, roll the pieces into equal sized balls, and place them sparsely on 2 baking trays lined with parchment paper. Flatten the balls slightly and bake them in the oven for approximately 10 minutes or until the cookies are golden. Let the cookies cool slightly and then move them to racks to cool completely. Keep in a dry place.

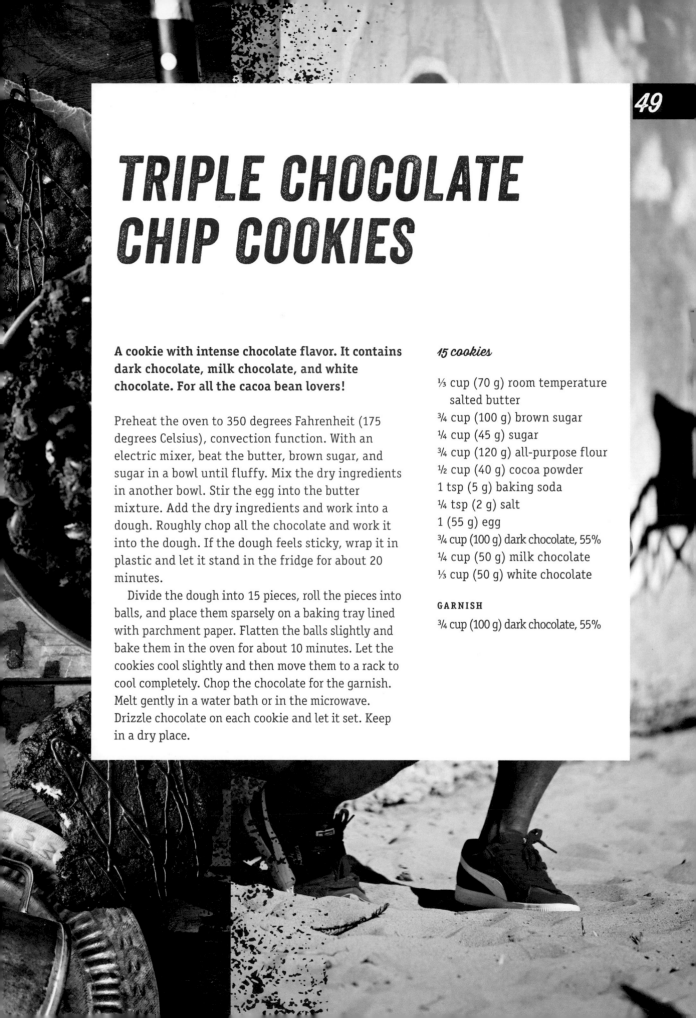

TRIPLE CHOCOLATE CHIP COOKIES

A cookie with intense chocolate flavor. It contains dark chocolate, milk chocolate, and white chocolate. For all the cacoa bean lovers!

Preheat the oven to 350 degrees Fahrenheit (175 degrees Celsius), convection function. With an electric mixer, beat the butter, brown sugar, and sugar in a bowl until fluffy. Mix the dry ingredients in another bowl. Stir the egg into the butter mixture. Add the dry ingredients and work into a dough. Roughly chop all the chocolate and work it into the dough. If the dough feels sticky, wrap it in plastic and let it stand in the fridge for about 20 minutes.

Divide the dough into 15 pieces, roll the pieces into balls, and place them sparsely on a baking tray lined with parchment paper. Flatten the balls slightly and bake them in the oven for about 10 minutes. Let the cookies cool slightly and then move them to a rack to cool completely. Chop the chocolate for the garnish. Melt gently in a water bath or in the microwave. Drizzle chocolate on each cookie and let it set. Keep in a dry place.

15 cookies

⅓ cup (70 g) room temperature salted butter
¾ cup (100 g) brown sugar
¼ cup (45 g) sugar
¾ cup (120 g) all-purpose flour
½ cup (40 g) cocoa powder
1 tsp (5 g) baking soda
¼ tsp (2 g) salt
1 (55 g) egg
¾ cup (100 g) dark chocolate, 55%
¼ cup (50 g) milk chocolate
⅓ cup (50 g) white chocolate

GARNISH
¾ cup (100 g) dark chocolate, 55%

GENEVA COOKIES

Fun and beautiful cookies that can be varied in all sorts of ways. It's quite easy to replace the nuts in the recipe with other types of nuts, crushed candy canes, salt flakes, sprinkles, M & M's, or other candy. Basically, anything you like!

COOKIES

Preheat the oven to 320 degrees Fahrenheit (160 degrees Celsius), convection function. With an electric mixer, whisk the butter, sugar, vanilla extract, and vinegar in a bowl until fluffy. Sift the dry ingredients in another bowl. Stir them into the butter mixture and work into a smooth dough. Place the dough on a floured work surface and roll out the dough into a ½ inch (4–5 mm) thick disk. Punch out 26 cookies with a round cutter, 2¾ inches (7 cm) in diameter.

Place the cookies on a baking sheet lined with parchment paper and bake in the oven for about 20 minutes. The cookies should have a light golden brown color. Let them cool completely.

GARNISH

Preheat oven to 400 degrees Fahrenheit (200 degrees Celsius). Roast all three nut varieties for 8–10 minutes in separate pans. Let them cool. Place the hazelnuts in a clean kitchen hand towel and rub off the shells. Coarsely chop the nuts.

Chop the chocolate and melt it gently in a water bath or in the microwave. Spread a layer of chocolate on each cookie with a small off-set spatula or the back of a spoon. Sprinkle the cookies with the different nuts and allow the chocolate to harden. Keep in a dry place.

26 cookies

COOKIES
¾ cup (200 g) room temperature salted butter
⅔ cup (140 g) sugar
½ tbsp (5 g) vanilla extract
1 tsp (5 g) white distilled vinegar
2 cups (270 g) all-purpose flour
1½ tsp (7 g) baking powder
½ tsp (2 g) baking soda

GARNISH
About ⅓ cup (50 g) hazelnuts
About ⅓ cup (50 g) pecans
About ⅓ cup (50 g) pistachios
2¼ cups (300 g) dark chocolate

BROWN SUGAR SHORTBREAD

To get straight and fine edges on these cookies, I let the rolled dough stand in the fridge before I cut it into rectangles. If you want to skip dipping the cookies in chocolate, that works just fine, as the cookies are amazingly good on their own. But one thing is certain—chocolate always makes things a little better. . .

20 cookies

1¼ cups (270 g) room temperature salted butter
½ cup (70 g) brown sugar
2¼ cups (300 g) all-purpose flour

GARNISH
½ cup (200 g) dark chocolate

Preheat the oven to 325 degrees Fahrenheit (165 degrees Celsius), convection function. Beat the butter and brown sugar in a bowl until fluffy, using an electric mixer. Add the flour and mix together into a dough. Place the dough on a floured work surface and work it until it becomes smooth. Add more flour if it feels sticky.

Cover a cutting board with lightly floured parchment paper. Roll out the dough into a rectangle, 10 × 5½ inches (25 x 14 cm), on top of the cutting board. Place the cutting board in the fridge for 20 minutes. Cut the rectangle into 20 rectangles, 1 × 2¾ inches (2½ x 7 cm).

Place the cookies on a baking sheet lined with parchment paper and prick them, for example, with a fork (I used the tip of my cooking thermometer). Bake the cookies in the oven for about 20 minutes. Allow to cool completely.

Chop the chocolate, put it in a bowl, and melt it gently in a water bath or in the microwave. Dip one end of each cookie in chocolate, place on a baking sheet, and let the chocolate harden. Keep in a dry place.

CHOCOLATE FUDGE

In my home country of Sweden, fudge is a treat reserved for Christmas time, but it really is something that can be enjoyed year round. So go on and eat more fudge! Caramelized milk is available in many grocery stores. If not, ask your grocer to order it. How could caramel sauce in a can do anything but sell well?

Approx. 50 pieces

3 cups (400 g) dark chocolate, 55 %
1 cup (100 g) walnuts
1¼ cups (270 g) sugar
1 can (about 400 g) dulce de leche sauce
¼ cup (60 g) butter
¾ tsp (5 g) salt
3 cups (140 g) mini marshmallows
½ tbsp (5 g) vanilla extract

Chop the chocolate and walnuts and place in a bowl. Grease the edges of a pan, 8 × 8 inches (21 x 21 cm), with vegetable oil and line the base with parchment paper.

Mix the sugar, caramelized milk, butter, and salt in a pan. Heat while constantly stirring the mixture until it just begins to simmer and the sugar has dissolved. Lower to medium heat, add the marshmallows, and stir until they have melted. Remove the pan from the heat, add the chocolate, walnuts, and vanilla and stir until the chocolate has melted.

Pour the mixture into the pan and let stand in the fridge for at least 5 hours. Turn out the fudge from the mold and cut into pieces; about 1 × 1 inches (3 cm x 3 cm). Let the fudge stand for 1–2 hours at room temperature so that it dries a little on the surface. Then store in a jar at room temperature.

ROCKY ROAD

When translated into Swedish, these stuffed chocolate bars would be called "bumpy road" and that's exactly what they are: whole nuts and large candy pieces. Here you can mix in almost anything that tastes delicious. You can make a slightly healthier version by just using roasted nuts.

Approx. 20 pieces

½ cup (70 g) peeled almonds
4¼ cups (550 g) dark chocolate, 55%
¾ cup (160 g) gumdrops
¾ cup (160 g) Peanut M & M's
1 cup (50 g) mini marshmallows
½ cup (60 g) dried cranberries

Preheat oven to 400 degrees Fahrenheit (200 degrees Celsius), convection function. Grease the edges of an oblong baking pan, 4½ × 10 inches (21 x 21 cm), with vegetable oil and line the base with parchment paper.

Put the almonds in a pan and roast them in the oven for 8–10 minutes. Chop the chocolate, put it in a bowl, and melt it gently in a water bath or in the microwave.

Mix all ingredients, except the chocolate, in a bowl. Add the chocolate and mix well.

Spread the mixture evenly in the pan and let stand in the fridge for at least 2 hours. Turn out from the mold, pull off the parchment paper, and let stand at room temperature for 10 minutes. Then divide into approximately 20 bits. Store in airtight container in the fridge, but serve warm or at room temperature.

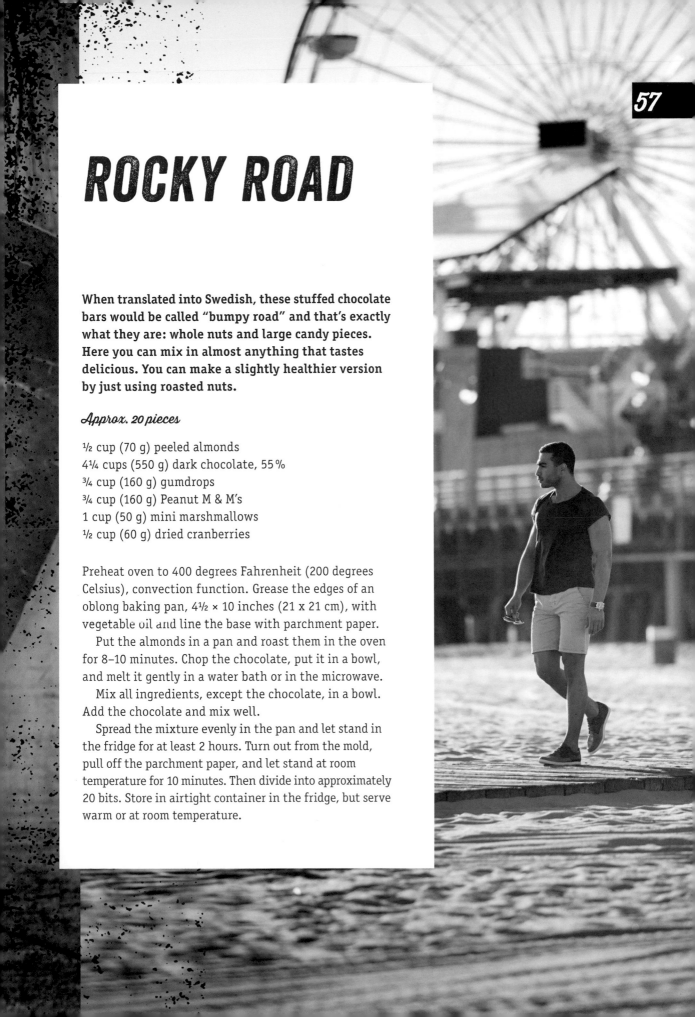

ICE CREAM SANDWICH

These super delicious ice cream sandwiches are a bit fussy to make, but guaranteed to be worthwhile. Invite your friends to try them, and I promise they'll be impressed that you made them yourself. Try wrapping them in waxed paper tied with a little string—both stylish and practical.

SOFT CHOCOLATE BISCUITS

Preheat the oven to 350 degrees Fahrenheit (175 degrees Celsius), convection function. Sift the flour and cacoa, into a bowl. Beat the butter, vanilla extract, sugar, and salt in a separate bowl until fluffy, using an electric mixer. Add the egg yolk together with the dry ingredients. Work into a smooth dough. Divide the dough into 2 equal pieces, wrap in plastic, and let rest in the fridge for 30 minutes.

Take out one piece of dough from the fridge and roll it out to a rectangle with a rolling pin, approximately 12 × 6 inches (30 x 15 cm). Cut the rectangle into about 4 × 2 inch (10 x 5 cm) biscuits and place them on a baking sheet lined with parchment paper. Repeat with the other chunk of dough and prick holes in the biscuits with a fork. Bake the biscuits in the oven for approximately 15 minutes. Allow to cool completely.

Let ice cream stand on a tray lined with parchment paper at room temperature for about 10 minutes or until it can be shaped. Spread the softened ice cream evenly into a parchment lined baking sheet and let it freeze for 2 hours.

Cut the ice cream rectangle into 4 × 2 inch (10 x 5 cm) pieces. Place the ice cream pieces between two biscuits, wrap in paper, and place in the freezer until ready to serve.

9 ice cream sandwiches

SOFT CHOCOLATE BISCUITS

1¼ cups (160 g) all-purpose flour

⅓ cup (30 g) cocoa powder

⅔ cup (150 g) room temperature unsalted butter

½ cup (90 g) sugar

¼ tbsp (2½ g) vanilla extract

¼ tsp (2 g) salt

1 (15 g) egg yolk

1 quart vanilla ice cream for the filling

JOAN'S ON THIRD

>> I love to visit the amazing gourmet market **Joan's on Third** (8350 West Third Street). The store, which is also a coffee shop with lighter fare, is imbued with a passion for quality and fine ingredients. Here, no detail has been overlooked, and sometimes I just stand and marvel at the beauty of all the sights and smells. So amazing! Many times I've wondered who Joan is? Just who is this brilliant person behind this operation? And now I know, for I finally managed to book a meeting with this very busy woman.

Joan gave me a warm welcome and told me about herself, how it was love that made her leave New York, where she ran both a culinary school and a restaurant, and how she moved to Los Angeles and started a family. In 1995, she launched Joan's on Third, initially only as a catering business. The company quickly earned a good reputation and many prestigious commissions from celebrities and the movie-world. Three years later, Joan turned her lifelong dream of opening a gourmet market with a café into a reality.

To hear Joan speak about her deep interest in baking was really something special. She spoke with such passion about menus, flavors, ingredients, cheeses, and wines that I completely forgot about the outside world for a while. But when she treated me to a Nutella-filled pop tart, I woke straight up. And it was so good that I asked for the recipe. I got it, and it appears on page 64. Try it out! I was honestly a little weak in the knees when I was with this charming and genuinely warm woman, and I really just wanted to hug her. When our meeting was over, I thanked her for the inspiring and interesting conversation and received my long-awaited hug.

JOAN'S NUTELLA POP TARTS

I enjoyed these delights when I visited my favorite café, Joan's on Third at 8350 West Third Street. I just had to ask for the recipe, so I could include it in the book.

DOUGH

Mix the flour, sugar, and salt in a food processor or in a bowl. Whisk together the egg and milk lightly in a bowl. Cut the butter into small cubes and work quickly, adding it into the flour mixture until it has become a crumbly dough. Add the liquid and work the dough quickly until it begins to come together. Divide the dough into 2 pieces; wrap them and place them in the fridge for 20 minutes.

FILLING

Chop the chocolate and melt it gently in a water bath or in the microwave. Add the Nutella, mix together, and set aside.

Preheat the oven to 350 degrees Fahrenheit (175 degrees Celsius), convection function. Remove one dough chunk out of the fridge and roll it with a rolling pin out into a rectangle, about 15½ × 7 inches (40 x 18 cm), on a floured work surface. Cut the rectangle into 16 rectangles, about 2 × 3½ inches (5 x 9 cm). Brush the rectangles lightly with the egg (helps to hold the top and bottom) and move them to a baking sheet lined with parchment paper.

Place 1 teaspoon of filling in center of each square, keeping the edges of the dough clean of excess filling. Roll out with a rolling pin and cut the other dough piece in the same way. Add the new rectangle on top of the filling, press the edges with a fork, and then prick the top side of each pop tart with a fork or toothpick.

Let the pop tarts stand in the freezer for about 20 minutes. Then bake the pop tarts in the oven for about 20 minutes or until they get a light color. Let cool completely on a wire rack. Store in a dry place.

16 pop tarts

DOUGH

2⅓ cups (330 g) all-purpose flour
1½ tbsp (20 g) sugar
¼ tsp (2 g) salt
1 (55 g) egg, lightly beaten
2 tbsp (29 mL (35 g)) milk
1 cup (220 g) cold unsalted butter

NUTELLA FILLING

¾ cup (100 g) dark chocolate, 55%
4 tbsp (100 g) Nutella

1 egg for brushing

BLUEBERRY BARS

A simple cookie that is quick to bake. The same dough used to make the bottom is crumbled on top. You basically just mix it all together and bake. The scent of blueberry that fills the kitchen from the freshly-baked bars is wonderful!

CRUMBLE

Preheat the oven to 350 degrees Fahrenheit (180 degrees Celsius), convection function. Grease the edges of a baking pan, 9 × 12 inches (22 cm x 30 cm), and line the base with parchment paper.

Cut the butter for the crumble into cubes and mix together with the sugar, flour, baking powder, eggs, and cinnamon in a bowl. Pinch with your fingertips together to form a crumble. Spread half of the mixture into the pan and smooth the surface.

BLUEBERRY FILLING

Stir together the sugar and cornstarch for the filling in a bowl. Mix the blueberries with the lemon zest and juice in a bowl. Fold in the sugar mixture and mix thoroughly. Divide the filling evenly in the pan and crumble over the rest of the dough. Bake in the oven for about 40 minutes, until the surface has a nice golden brown color.

When cool, cut into squares and store in a dry place. If you like, serve with vanilla ice cream.

24 pieces

CRUMBLE

¾ cup (200 g) salted butter
1 cup (210 g) sugar
2⅔ cups (375 g)
    all-purpose flour
1 tsp (5 g) baking powder
1 (55 g) egg
1 tsp (2 g) ground
    cinnamon

BLUEBERRY FILLING

½ cup + 1 tbsp (100 g)
    sugar
1 tbsp (8 g) cornstarch
1 lb (500 g) fresh
    blueberries
1 lemon, zest from the
    whole lemon and juice
    from half the lemon.

Optional: vanilla ice
    cream for serving

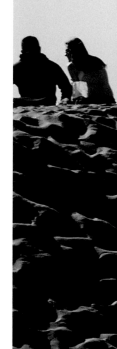

CAKES, PIES, *and* CHEESE CAKES

Downtown Los Angeles is actually a business district with tall skyscrapers and public administration buildings. The area is quite small if you look at Los Angeles as a whole. To make the area feel more alive, the city has been trying for some time to attract more people to move here by rebuilding. More and more office buildings have been converted into homes in hopes of creating a more attractive neighborhood to live in.

When I want to experience a bit of the big city life, I head downtown. Here, the pace is fast. Tons of taxis, energy, and vibrancy in the air. It feels like the word "business" really applies here. My favorite place is **Bottega Louie** (700 South Grand Avenue)—a stunning food temple that includes a restaurant, bar, and patisserie.

DOWNTOW

FLAG CAKE

The Fourth of July is a national holiday, celebrated with pomp and circumstance. Everyone really goes all out, adorning American flags everywhere and devoting the entire day to celebrating. During my travels, I've experienced this holiday several times, and I'm always happy when I see how proud people are of their country. I think my fellow Swedes ought to take this as an example and celebrate our national holiday. After all, we have much to be proud of.

CAKE BOTTOM

Preheat the oven to 350 degrees Fahrenheit (175 degrees Celsius), convection function. Grease and lightly flour the edges of a baking pan, 13 × 9 inches (33 cm x 22 cm), and line the base with parchment paper.

Mix the milk and vinegar in a bowl. Sift all the dry ingredients in another bowl. Beat the butter, vanilla extract, and sugar in a separate bowl until fluffy. Mix in 1 egg at a time. Stir in the dry ingredients little by little. Finally, add the milk mixture and lemon zest and mix well.

Spread batter evenly in pan and bake in middle of the oven for about 40 minutes. Use a toothpick to check that the cake is baked through. Let cool and then turn it out of the form. Optionally, even the sides using a sharp knife.

FROSTING

Beat the cream cheese and butter until fluffy. Beat in the vanilla, icing sugar, and lemon zest. Add the cream and whisk together into a fine and firm frosting.

Spread the frosting evenly over the cake. Decorate with berries of your choice, or do as I have done and use raspberries and blueberries. For white berries, set dry berries onto the cake first and dust with powdered sugar, then add the rest of the berries.

Approx. 20 slices

CAKE BOTTOM
2 cups (435 mL (450 g)) room temperature whole milk
2 tbsp (30 mL (20 g)) white distilled vinegar
3¼ cups (450 g) all-purpose flour
⅓ cup (40 g) cornstarch
2 tsp (10 g) baking powder
1 tsp (5 g) baking soda
1 tsp (7 g) salt
1 cup (230 g) room temperature salted butter
1 tsp (3 g) vanilla extract
1¾ cups (380 g) sugar
4 (220 g) eggs, room temperature
Grated zest of 1 lemon

FROSTING
1¼ cups (300 g) cream cheese
¼ cup (50 g) room temperature unsalted butter
½ tsp (2½ g) vanilla extract
1⅔ cups (240 g) powdered sugar
Grated zest of 1 lemon
¼ cup (59 mL (50 g)) whipping cream

GARNISH
Fresh berries (for example, raspberries and blueberries)

DEVIL'S FOOD CHOCOLATE CAKE

If the mousse is too loose when you assemble the cake, just let it stand and solidify a while in the fridge.

CAKE LAYERS

Preheat the oven to 300 degrees Fahrenheit (150 degrees Celsius), convection function. Grease and flour the edges of 3 springform pans, 8½ inches (22 cm) in diameter. Line the bottoms with parchment paper. Sift the dry ingredients in a bowl. Whisk together eggs, vanilla extract, milk, and oil lightly in another bowl. Mix the dry ingredients into the egg mixture and stir in the water.

Spread the batter into the molds and bake in the oven for approximately 50 minutes. Use a toothpick to be sure the layers are baked through. Let them cool completely and then remove them from the molds.

CHOCOLATE BUTTER CREAM

Beat the butter and vanilla extract in a bowl until fluffy with an electric mixer. Chop the chocolate and melt it gently in a water bath or in the microwave. Let it cool to a lukewarm temperature.

Beat the egg whites, sugar, and salt by hand in a water bath until the sugar is dissolved. Remove from heat and continue to whisk, with an electric mixer, until the meringue is cool. Whisk in the butter and chocolate in batches. Let stand at room temperature.

DARK CHOCOLATE MOUSSE

Beat one ⅔ cup serving of cream and set it in the fridge. Chop the chocolate and place it in a bowl. Bring the other ⅔ cup of cream to a boil and pour it into the bowl with the chocolate. Let it stand for a bit, then mix with a spatula into a smooth ganache. Let stand at room temperature.

Place the egg yolks in a bowl. Bring the sugar and water to a boil and whisk with an electric mixer at maximum speed, immediately pouring the syrup in a thin stream into the egg yolks. Fold in the ganache and then add the ⅔ cup of cream from the fridge.

Pipe an approximately one half-inch (1 cm) wide rim of buttercream along the edge of each layer and spread the mousse inside the buttercream rim. Add the layers together and cover the entire cake with buttercream. Decorate with piped buttercream and let stand in refrigerator for at least 3 hours.

Approx. 14 slices

CAKE LAYERS

2⅓ cups (330 g) all-purpose flour
2¼ cups (450 g) sugar
1¼ cups (120 g) cocoa powder
2 tsp (10 g) baking soda
2 tsp (10 g) baking powder
1½ tsp (10 g) salt
3 eggs (165 g), room temperature
¾ tbsp (6 g) vanilla extract
1½ cups (355 mL) room temperature milk
¾ cup (190 mL) vegetable oil
1¼ cups (295 mL (300 g)) boiling water

CHOCOLATE BUTTER CREAM

1¾ cups (400 g) room temperature, unsalted butter
½ tbsp (5 g) vanilla extract
2¼ cups (300 g) dark chocolate, 70%
4 (150 g) egg whites
1 cup (220 g) sugar
1 pinch of salt

DARK CHOCOLATE MOUSSE

⅔ cup (157 mL) whipping cream
1 cup (150 g) dark chocolate, 70%
2 servings of whipping cream, ⅔ cup (157 mL) each
2 (30 g) egg yolks
2 tbsp (30 g) sugar
1 tbsp (15 g) water

MAGNOLIA BAKERY

>> The first thing that greets me when I come through the door is the lovely smell of freshly baked cookies and cupcakes. Wonderful! It is here, in the almost legendary **Magnolia Bakery** (8389 West Third Street), where I'll spend the day observing and learning more about baking cakes.

The first Magnolia Bakery opened in 1996 by married couple Steve and Tyra Abrams in New York. The idea was to bake classic American cakes and serve them in a vintage-style shop. The bakery was a success and there are now seven branches in the United States. Magnolia Bakery also received international attention when it appeared in the TV series *Sex and the City* and has since appeared in several films and TV series.

Marissa Perez, who oversees cake decoration, welcomed me right away and showed me around. Everybody works behind a tall glass window at the store, so that it becomes a bit of a baking show in there. One person makes the cake layers, one makes fillings and frostings, one decorates, and then everyone changes workstations with each other about once a week.

At first I just stood and watched in order to learn how she worked. I took the opportunity to ask her about various frostings and techniques—and, in particular, how they get their pastries to be so moist. Here are some good tips: baking powder must be fresh, the ingredients should be room temperature, the butter should be whipped really fluffy, and oven temperature should be adjusted according to how the batter is tempered. This last one can be a bit tricky, but basically it means that a cooler batter should have a slightly higher starting temperature than a batter that is a little warmer.

Then, it was time for me to show what I could do. Especially after having boasted about my last book *Sweet!* and my TV shows, I felt somewhat nervous. Time to prove it! I grabbed a palette knife and the first thing Marissa did was correct the angle at which I was holding it. So things definitely started off well. . . After a few tries, I got the hang of it with the palette knife while I spun the turntable (laughing while doing this was probably not the best idea, but of course I did in the beginning). But remember: Frosting is easy to remove, so you can start over.

After an exceptionally pleasant day, I left Magnolia Bakery, very satisfied and very full. I met wonderful people and was reminded of the old adage that practice makes perfect!

MAGNOLIA BAKERY'S BANANA CAKE

Inspired by my study-visit at Magnolia Bakery, I put together this cake with banana and butterscotch. Bananas make cake super moist. And butterscotch cream is beyond delicious!

CAKE LAYERS

Preheat the oven to 275 degrees Fahrenheit (140 degrees Celsius), convection function. Grease and flour the edges of three baking pans, about 8½ inches (21–22 cm) in diameter. Line the bottoms with parchment paper. Mash the bananas, mix in the lemon juice, and zest. Sift the flour and baking soda in a bowl. Mix the milk and vinegar in a bowl. Beat the butter, vanilla extract, and sugar in a bowl until fluffy. Stir 1 egg at a time into the butter mixture. Whisk the dry ingredients in batches with the milk mixture. Add bananas and mix well.

Spread the batter evenly into the molds and bake for approximately 40 minutes. Use a toothpick to test that the layers are baked through. Let the layers cool. Optionally, even out the sides using a sharp knife.

BUTTERSCOTCH CREAM

Beat the butter in a bowl until fluffy. Whisk the egg whites in a separate bowl until they form stiff peaks. Bring the water and sugar to a boil at 250 degrees Fahrenheit (121 degrees Celsius). Check the temperature with a candy thermometer. Immediately pour the syrup in a thin stream down into the egg whites and whisk together with a hand mixer at maximum speed. Then whisk on medium speed until the meringue is cold. Stir in the butter in batches. Mix in the caramelized milk and stir to form a smooth cream.

Assemble the cake with caramel cream between the layers. Cover the whole cake with the rest of the cream, and if you like, pipe patterns. I used the star-shaped tip when I piped.

12–14 slices

CAKE LAYERS
4 bananas
2 tsp (10 g) lemon juice + zest from half a lemon
3¼ cups (460 g) all-purpose flour
2 tsp (10 g) baking soda
1¼ cups (295 mL (300 g)) room temperature whole milk
1½ tsp (8 g) white distilled vinegar
¾ cup (180 g) room temperature salted butter
½ tbsp (5 g) vanilla extract
2¼ cups (470 g) sugar
3 (165 g) eggs, room temperature

BUTTERSCOTCH CREAM
3¼ cups (750 g) room temperature unsalted butter
4 (150 g) egg whites
½ cup (118 mL (100 g)) water
1⅓ cups (300 g) sugar
Approx. 2 cans (800 g) dulce de leche

SUMMER BERRY CAKE

A summery cake with delicious flavors of vanilla and fresh berries that nicely contrasts the chocolate cake. Works really well at a summer party because it can sit out for a bit without going bad.

CAKE LAYERS

Preheat the oven to 300 degrees Fahrenheit (150 degrees Celsius), convection function. Grease and lightly flour the edges of four baking molds, 8½ inches (21–22 cm) in diameter. Line the bottoms with parchment paper. Sift all the dry ingredients in a bowl. In another bowl, lightly whisk together by hand the eggs, vanilla extract, milk, and oil. Stir together the dry ingredients and the egg mixture and mix to a smooth batter. Add the water and mix together to form a loose batter.

Spread the batter into the molds and bake in the oven for about 40 minutes. Use a toothpick to test that the layers are baked through. Let the layers cool. Optionally, even out the sides with a sharp knife.

BUTTERCREAM

Using an electric mixer, beat the butter and vanilla extract in a bowl until fluffy. Whisk the egg whites, sugar, and salt by hand in a water bath until the sugar is dissolved. Remove the bowl from the heat and continue to whip with an electric mixer, until the meringue is cool. Add a little at a time to the butter and whisk until it becomes a smooth and delicate cream.

MASCARPONE FILLING

Whisk together the mascarpone, powdered sugar, and vanilla extract lightly in a bowl. Stir in the cream a little at a time. Beat until it becomes a nice and firm cream. Finally, mix in the lemon zest. Cut the berries that will be inside the cake into small pieces. Assemble the cake with mascarpone cream and berry pieces between the layers. Cover the whole cake with buttercream and decorate with berries.

12–14 slices

CAKE LAYERS
2⅓ cups (330 g) all-purpose flour
2⅓ cups (510 g) sugar
1¼ cups (120 g) cocoa powder
1 tbsp (15 g) baking soda
1½ tsp (7 g) baking powder
1½ tsp (10 g) salt
3 (165 g) eggs, room temperature
1½ cups (355 mL (350 g)) room temperature milk
½ tbsp (5 g) vanilla extract
¾ cup (177 mL (180 g)) vegetable oil
1½ cups (355 mL (350 g)) boiling water

BUTTERCREAM
1¾ cups (400 g) room temperature unsalted butter
½ tbsp (5 g) vanilla extract
4 (150 g) egg whites
1 cup (220 g) sugar
1 pinch salt

MASCARPONE FILLING
1 lbs (500 g) mascarpone cheese
1 cup (150 g) powdered sugar
1 tbsp (8 g) vanilla extract
1 cup (237mL (250 g)) whipping cream
Grated zest from one lemon
Approx. 4 cups fresh berries

GARNISH
Fresh berries

ESPRESSO CAKE

An amazingly good cake! The combination of chocolate, coffee, and marshmallow is tough to beat.

CAKE LAYERS

Preheat the oven to 310 degrees Fahrenheit (155 degrees Celsius), convection function. Grease and lightly flour the edges of four baking molds, 8 ¼ inch (21–22 cm) in diameter. Line the bottoms with parchment paper. Sift all the dry ingredients in a bowl. Lightly whisk together the eggs, vanilla extract, milk, and oil in another bowl. Stir the dry ingredients into the egg mixture and stir together until smooth. Add the coffee and mix well.

Spread the batter into the molds and bake in the oven for approximately 40 minutes. Use a toothpick to test that the layers are baked through. Let the layers cool completely and then remove them from the molds.

COFFEE BUTTERCREAM

Chop the chocolate and melt it gently in a water bath or in the microwave. Allow to cool to a lukewarm temperature. Beat the butter and vanilla extract with an electric mixer in a bowl until fluffy. Beat the egg whites, sugar, and salt by hand in a water bath until the sugar has dissolved. Remove from heat and continue to whisk, with an electric mixer, until the meringue is cool. Whisk in the butter and chocolate in batches. Add half of the coffee and mix thoroughly. Taste and add more coffee for a stronger flavor.

MARSHMALLOW FILLING

Beat the butter, powdered sugar, and vanilla extract with an electric mixer in a bowl until fluffy. Add the marshmallow fluff and whisk together until a smooth filling. Spread half of the marshmallow filling evenly over a cake layer. Add the next layer and spread buttercream evenly over it. Add the third layer and spread out the rest of the marshmallow filling. Add the last layer, cover the cake with butter cream, and garnish with Whoppers. Let stand in refrigerator for at least three hours, and at room temperature for 30 minutes before serving.

12–14 slices

CAKE LAYERS

2⅓ cups (330 g) all-purpose flour
2⅓ cups (510 g) sugar
1¼ cups (120 g) cocoa powder
1 tbsp (15 g) baking soda
1½ tsp (7 g) baking powder
1½ tsp (10 g) salt
½ tbsp (5 g) vanilla extract
3 (165 g) eggs, room temperature
1½ cups (355 mL (350 g)) room temperature milk
¾ cup (177 mL (180 g)) vegetable oil
1½ cups (355 mL (350 g)) hot, brewed coffee

COFFEE BUTTERCREAM

1½ cups (200 g) dark chocolate, 70%
1¾ cups (400 g) room temperature unsalted butter
1¼ tsp (4 g) vanilla extract
4 (150 g) egg whites
1 cup (220 g) sugar
1 pinch salt
⅓ cup (79 mL (75 g)) lukewarm espresso

MARSHMALLOW FILLING

1 cup + 2 tbsp (250 g) room temperature unsalted butter
¾ cup (120 g) powdered sugar
½ tsp (2½ g) vanilla extract
8 oz (ca 210 g) marshmallow fluff

GARNISH

1–2 bags Whoppers (malted milk balls)

HOLLYWOOD

>> Hollywood, as everyone knows, is the heart of the film industry in the United States. To some extent, this is still the case but most major movie studios have moved to other neighborhoods. Many premiere theaters remain, however, and it is home to the Hollywood Walk of Fame with the names of countless movie stars in each slab of sidewalk.

Hollywood and West Hollywood are primarily what Los Angeles means to me. The architecture varies wildly, and I'm totally in love with the mixture of the styles of the houses. Here there are no high-rises, only small cozy neighborhoods with cafes, shops, and street life. My favorite coffee shop, called Sweet Lady Jane, is located in West Hollywood.

SWEET LADY JANE

>> **Jane Lockhart** grew tired of all the over-sweetened baked goods made from artificial ingredients and founded the cake shop, **Sweet Lady Jane** (8360 Melrose Avenue), in 1988. Here, things are baked only with genuine ingredients of high quality and no preservatives or other additives are used.

For me, Sweet Lady Jane symbolizes a love for the authentic, especially when it comes to baked goods. But this also applies to the furnishings and design. It's cozy, simple, and rustic with a little hint of New England.

When I visited the bakery recently with my friend Tanja Djelevic, I tried their red velvet cake. Totally fabulous! (See the next page for my own variation on the recipe.) Tanja lives year-round in LA and works as a personal trainer. Since I'm also interested in training and health—combined with my sweet life—we have a lot in common. And have a lot of fun together!

RED VELVET CAKE

You see this lovely cake everywhere. Red Velvet cake is a red chocolate cake with cream cheese frosting originally from the South. Don't be stingy with the food coloring here. If you want to bring out the red color, it requires the amount specified.

CAKE LAYERS

Preheat the oven to 325 degrees Fahrenheit (160 degrees Celsius), convection function. Grease and lightly flour edges of three baking molds, 8½ inches (22 cm) in diameter, and line the bottoms with parchment paper.

Combine the milk, vanilla extract, 1½ tbsp of vinegar, and the red food coloring in a bowl. Mix the flour, sugar, cocoa powder, and salt in stand mixer with the beater blade attachment or use and electric hand mixer on low speed. Add the butter and work for 5 minutes on low speed. Then add the milk mixture in batches and then 1 egg at a time. Mix until it becomes a smooth and fine batter. Scrape the edges in between. Combine the baking soda and 1 tsp of vinegar in a bowl, pour this down into the batter and mix well.

Spread the batter evenly into the molds and bake in the middle of the oven for about 45 minutes. Use a toothpick to test that the layers are baked through. Let them cool completely. Optionally, smooth the side of the layers with a sharp knife.

FROSTING

Beat the butter in a bowl until fluffy. Add the cream cheese and continue to whisk until it becomes a smooth mixture. Add in the vanilla extract and powdered sugar and whisk vigorously until the frosting is nice and firm.

Assemble the cake with frosting between the layers. Cover the whole cake with the rest of the frosting. If the frosting feels too loose, set it in the freezer for a short while.

12–14 slices

CAKE LAYERS

1½ cups (355 mL (350 g)) of room temperature whole milk

½ tbsp (5 g) vanilla extract

1½ tbsp (22 mL (20 g)) white distilled vinegar

⅓ cup (79 mL (75 g)) of red food coloring

3⅓ cups (480 g) all-purpose flour

2¼ cups (450 g) sugar

⅓ cup (30 g) cocoa powder

1½ tsp (10 g) salt

¾ cup (170 g) room temperature unsalted butter

3 (165 g) eggs, room temperature

1½ tsp (7 g) baking soda

1½ tsp (5 mL (10 g)) white distilled vinegar

FROSTING

½ cup (110 g) room temperature unsalted butter

2½ cups (600 g) cream cheese

½ tbsp (5 g) vanilla extract

3⅓ cups (480 g) powdered sugar

Bountiful (1335 Abbot Kinney Boulevard) is a very special shop owned by **Sue Balmforth.** This boutique is literally brimming with antiques, vintage and modern interior design details—all displayed in a unique way. I lose my breath every time I walk into this paradise, for among all the incredibly beautiful things, there are numerous pie and cake stands piled up to the ceiling (but then I have to take an extra deep breath to keep from stumbling!) Sue sells almost exclusively domestically produced cake stands—she takes pride in simply buying from small producers around the country, which means that prices also reflect this. But I still can't help but fall for at least one cake stand each time I visit.

KEY LIME PIE

The name of this bright and fresh pie is taken from a particular type of lime, the Key lime. It has a distinct taste—a variety a little more sour than the usual lime—and it used to be grown in large amounts in the island chain known as the Florida Keys. About 5 regular limes yields about 125 grams of lime juice. Feel free to use Key limes, but it tastes just as good with regular limes.

PIE SHELL
Preheat the oven to 350 degrees Fahrenheit (180 degrees Celsius), convection function. Melt the butter. Blend the crackers well in a food processor and combine with the sugar in a bowl. Add the butter and mix thoroughly. Line 8 pie molds with removable edges, 2¾ inches (7 cm) in diameter, with the mixture. Bake in the oven for 8 minutes. Let the pie shells cool completely.

LIME FILLING
Preheat the oven to 340 degrees Fahrenheit (170 degrees Celsius), convection function. Mix with a spatula the condensed milk, lime juice, lime zest, and vanilla extract in a bowl. Fold in the egg yolks and then the eggs. Stir gently together into a smooth mixture. Let the mixture stand and infuse for 15 minutes, strain out the lime zest, and then pour the filling into the molds.

Bake in the oven for about 10 minutes. Let cool completely and top with soft whipped cream and lime slices.

8 slices

PIE SHELL
⅓ cup + 1 tbsp (100 g) salted butter
15 (200 g) graham crackers
2 tbsp (30 g) sugar

LIME FILLING
1 can (ca 400 g) sweetened condensed milk
½ (118 mL (125 g)) squeezed lime juice + zest of two limes
½ tbsp (5 g) vanilla extract
2 (30 g) egg yolks
2 (110 g) eggs

GARNISH
1¼ cups (300 g) whipping cream
Thin lime slices

PUMPKIN PIE

Pumpkin pie is traditionally served on Thanksgiving. You can find pumpkin purée in fine grocery stores, or easily make your own purée. Boil or bake the pumpkin pieces until soft and blend them into a purée.

PIE SHELL

Mix the dry ingredients in a food processor. Cut the butter into small cubes and let them sit in the freezer for 15 minutes, making sure they are not completely frozen solid. Remove them from the fridge and put them in the food processor. Use the pulse button until the mixture begins to crumble. Add the water a little at a time and run until the dough just begins to come together but not more. The dough can also be worked up quickly by hand in a bowl. Wrap the dough in plastic and let it sit in the fridge for 30–40 minutes.

Roll out the dough into a ¼ inch (3–4 mm) thick disk and line a pie plate, 9½ inches (24 cm) in diameter, with the dough. Make sure the dough comes up over the edges of the form, and then cut off the excess. Let stand in the freezer for one hour. During this time, preheat the oven to 350 degrees Fahrenheit (180 degrees Celsius), convection function.

Cover pie crust with aluminum foil and fill it with dried peas. The peas make sure that the sides don't collapse when pre-baking the shell (they can be reused later). Bake in the oven for about 18 minutes.

PUMPKIN FILLING

Preheat the oven to 350 degrees Fahrenheit (170 degrees Celsius), convection function. Melt the butter. Whisk together the cream cheese, pumpkin purée, and sugar lightly in a bowl. Add the vanilla extract. Whisk in the cream and butter in batches. Also add in the egg and egg yolks in batches and whisk until the mixture becomes smooth and fine. Mix in the spices and pour the filling into the pie shell. Smooth with a spatula.

Bake in oven for 45–50 minutes. Let pie cool completely at room temperature. Serve with a dollop of lightly whipped cream.

10–12 slices

PIE SHELL

1¼ cups (180 g) all-purpose flour
½ tsp (3 g) salt
1 tbsp (12 g) sugar
½ cup (110 g) ice-cold unsalted butter
2 tbsp (30 mL (25 g)) ice-cold water

PUMPKIN FILLING

¼ cup (50 g) salted butter
1¼ cups (300 g) cream cheese
One 15 oz can (425 g) pumpkin purée
1 cup (220 g) sugar
½ tsp vanilla extract
¾ cup (177 mL (200 g)) whipping cream
1 (55 g) egg
2 (30 g) egg yolks
1 tbsp (7 g) ground cinnamon
1 tsp (2 g) ground ginger

1¼ cups (295 mL (300 g)) whipping cream for serving

SALTED CARAMEL CHOCOLATE TART

Yes, I confess. I'm a fiend for caramel. And there's nothing else to say other than that this is a crazy good pie.

PIE SHELL

Preheat the oven to 350 degrees Fahrenheit (180 degrees Celsius), convection function. Mix the flour and cocoa powder in a bowl. Beat the butter, vanilla extract, and powdered sugar until fluffy in a separate bowl. Whisk in the egg yolk and add the dry ingredients. Work into a dough, wrap it in plastic, and let it rest in the fridge for 30 minutes.

Roll out the dough on a floured work surface to a ¼ inch (3–4 mm) thick disk. Line a square baking tin with a detachable edge, 8½ × 8½ inches (22 x 22 cm),round shape, 9½ inches (24 cm) in diameter with the dough. The dough will come over the edges, so remove the excess by cutting it away. Prick the bottom with a fork and let the pie crust stand in the freezer for 15 minutes. Bake in the oven for 15 minutes. Allow to cool completely.

CARAMEL FILLING

Heat the cream, butter, and vanilla extract in a saucepan until the butter has melted. Set aside. In another pan, bring the corn syrup to a boil. In batches, stir the sugar and salt into the corn syrup. Carefully bring to a boil at 350 degrees Fahrenheit (170 degrees Celsius). Check the temperature with a candy thermometer. Stir occasionally.

Stir in the cream mixture a little at a time and boil until it is 250 degrees Fahrenheit (123 degrees Celsius). Stir occasionally. Pour the filling in the mold and let it cool completely at room temperature.

CHOCOLATE TRUFFLE

Chop the chocolate and place in a bowl. Bring the cream to a boil and pour it over the chocolate. Let stand for one minute and then mix with a spatula into a smooth truffle. Cover the bowl with plastic and let the truffle cool for 30 minutes. Spread the caramel truffle over the shell, sprinkle with a little sea salt, and let the pie stand in the fridge for at least 2 hours before serving.

10–12 slices

PIE SHELL

¾ cup (120 g) all-purpose flour
4 tbsp (25 g) cocoa powder
½ cup (100 g) room temperature salted butter
⅓ cup (45 g) powdered sugar
1 (15 g) egg yolk
¼ tsp (1 g) vanilla extract

CARAMEL FILLING

1¼ cups (300 g) whipping cream
½ cup + 1 tsp (120 g) salted butter
¼ tbsp (2½ g) vanilla extract
⅔ cup (157 mL (250 g)) corn syrup
2 cups (410 g) sugar
1½ tsp (10 g) salt

CHOCOLATE TRUFFLE

1 cup (120 g) dark chocolate
½ cup (118 mL (125 g)) whipping cream

Flaked salt for sprinkling

CHEESECAKE IN A JAR

Super easy, quick to make, and the perfect thing to take to a party or picnic. The recipe works just as well with other types of berries if you want to try something besides strawberries.

Approx. 8 portions

CRUMBLE DOUGH
12 (150 g) graham crackers
¼ cup (45 g) sugar
⅓ cup (90 g) room
   temperature salted butter
¼ cup (30 g) all-purpose flour
½ tsp (3 g) baking powder
¼ tbsp (2½ g) vanilla extract

CHEESECAKE FILLING
1¼ cups (300 g) cream cheese
¼ cup (45 g) sugar
1 cup (237 mL (250 g))
   whipping cream
1 tsp (2½ g) vanilla extract
Grated zest and juice from one
   lemon
20 fresh strawberries

CRUMBLE DOUGH
Preheat the oven to 350 degrees Fahrenheit (180 degrees Celsius), convection function. Run the cookies in a food processor until they become fine crumbs. Pour the crumbs into a bowl and add the sugar, butter, flour, baking powder, and vanilla extract. Pinch into a crumbly dough.

Sprinkle the dough on a baking sheet with parchment paper and bake in the center of the oven for about 10 minutes. Allow to cool completely.

CHEESECAKE FILLING
Beat the cream cheese and sugar until fluffy with an electric mixer in a bowl. Whisk in the cream little by little. Add the vanilla extract, lemon zest, and lemon juice and whisk until the cream is airy and smooth.

Divide the strawberries into pieces. Layer the crumble, cheesecake filling, and strawberries in jars, glasses, or bowls.

MICHIGAN APPLE PIE

In order to make a fine and crispy pie dough, the ingredients need to be as cold as possible. And be sure not to overwork the dough, otherwise it will be chewy and dull.

PIE DOUGH

Mix the dry ingredients in a food processor. Cut the butter into small cubes and let them sit in the freezer for 15 minutes, making sure they do not become frozen solid. Remove them from the fridge and add them to the food processor. Use the pulse function to blend until the mixture becomes crumbly. Add the water a little at a time and run until dough starts to come together. Not more. The dough can also be quickly worked together by hand in a bowl.

Divide the dough into two pieces and wrap them in plastic wrap. Let rest in the refrigerator for at least 3 hours. Then roll out one piece of dough into a ¼ inch (3 mm) thick disk and line a pie dish, 9½ inches (24 cm) in diameter, with the dough. There will be about a one inch overhang of dough when lining the dish. Cut off the excess dough with scissors.

APPLE FILLING

Preheat the oven to 425 degrees Fahrenheit (220 degrees Celsius), convection function. Peel, core, and cut the apples into very thin wedges. Place the wedges in the pie pan. Mix the flour, cornstarch, and cinnamon in a bowl. Put the butter, vanilla extract, sugar, and brown sugar in a pan. Add the water and heat until the butter and sugar have dissolved. Whisk the dry ingredients in batches into the pan. Let simmer, stirring until the mixture has thickened a little. Drizzle the mixture over the apple wedges.

Whisk together the egg yolk and cream and brush onto the edges of the dough. Roll out the second dough piece to about the same size as the former. Apply as a cover, press gently along the edge with a fork, and cut off the excess dough. Cut a few incisions in the dough cover to allow steam to escape.

Bake pie in middle of the oven for 15 minutes. Reduce heat to 350 degrees Fahrenheit (180 degrees Celsius) and bake for about another 50 minutes or until the pie is golden. Let the pie cool completely and then serve with vanilla ice cream.

10–12 slices

PIE DOUGH
2½ cups (360 g) all-purpose flour
¼ tsp (2 g) salt
2 tbsp (18 g) powdered sugar
1 cup + 2 tbsp (260 g) freezer-cold unsalted butter
⅓ cup (79 mL (50 g)) ice-cold water

APPLE FILLING
7 large Granny Smith apples
3 tbsp (30 g) all-purpose flour
1 tbsp (10 g) corn starch
1½ tsp (3 g) ground cinnamon
½ cup (110 g) unsalted butter
⅔ cup (120 g) sugar
½ cup (70 g) brown sugar
½ tsp (2 g) vanilla extract
¼ cup (59 mL (50 g)) water

BRUSHING
1 (15 g) egg yolk
1 tbsp (15 g) whipping cream

1 quart vanilla ice cream for serving

CHOCOLATE CREAM PIES

People are imaginative and will happily create things with their favorite ingredients—here, those would be chocolate and cream.

PIE SHELLS

Mix the flour and cocoa powder in a small bowl. In another bowl whisk the butter, vanilla extract, and powdered sugar until fluffy. Whisk in the yolk and add the dry ingredients. Work it together into a dough, wrap the dough in plastic and let it rest in the refrigerator for 30 minutes. During that time, preheat the oven to 350 degrees Fahrenheit (180 degrees Celsius), convection function.

Roll the dough on a floured work surface to a ¼ inch (3 mm) thick disk. Line seven pie dishes with loose, detachable rims and a diameter of 3 inches (8 cm), with the dough. Line the molds with dough up to the top edges and cut away excess dough with a knife. Prick the bottoms with a fork and let the pastry shells stand in the freezer for 15 minutes. Bake in the center of the oven for about 13 minutes. Let the shells cool completely and then gently pull them out of the molds.

Chop the chocolate and melt it gently in a water bath or in the microwave. Brush the insides of the pie shells with chocolate and let it set.

CHOCOLATE CREAM

Chop the chocolate and place in a bowl. Mix egg yolks, sugar, cornstarch, and vanilla extract in another bowl. Bring the milk to a boil and stir it in well into the egg mixture. Pour everything back into the saucepan and heat on medium heat, stirring continuously until the mixture thickens to a cream.

Pour the cream over the chocolate, add in the butter, and stir until the chocolate and butter have melted. Cover with plastic wrap and let stand at room temperature until the cream has cooled completely.

Spread the cream in the pastry shells, cover the pies with plastic wrap, and let them stand in the fridge for at least 5 hours. When serving, garnish the pies with soft whipped cream and shaved chocolate, and dust with the cocoa powder.

7 portions of pie

PIE SHELL

¾ cup (120 g) all-purpose flour
4 tbsp (25 g) cocoa powder
⅓ tsp (1 g) vanilla extract
½ cup (100 g) room temperature salted butter
⅓ cup (45 g) powdered sugar
1 (15 g) egg yolk
¼ cup (50 g) dark chocolate, 70%, for brushing

CHOCOLATE CREAM

¾ cup (100 g) dark chocolate, 70%
4 (60 g) egg yolks
⅓ cup (75 g) sugar
2½ tbsp (20 g)corn starch
½ tsp (1½ g) vanilla extract
1½ cups (355 mL (350 g)) whole milk
2 tbsp (20 g) unsalted butter

GARNISH

1¼ cups (295 mL (300 g)) whipping cream
¼ cup (50 g) dark chocolate shavings, 70%
Cocoa powder for dusting

SNICKERS CHEESECAKE

If I could only eat one pie for the rest of my life, I would choose this one. It's so incredibly good!

PIE SHELL

Preheat the oven to 350 degrees Fahrenheit (180 degrees Celsius), convection function. Run the cookies in a food processor until they become fine crumbs. Melt the butter and add it. Add a little more butter if you think that the mixture is too dry to work with. Line a springform, 9 inches (23 cm) in diameter, with the crumbs, create an edge of about 1½ inches (4 cm) high. Flatten the surface a little with the back of a tablespoon. Bake in the center of the oven for 7 minutes. Allow to cool.

CHEESECAKE FILLING

Preheat the oven to 400 degrees Fahrenheit (200 degrees Celsius), convection function. Beat the cream cheese, sugar, vanilla extract, and flour in a bowl until fluffy. Whisk in the cream. Fold in the egg yolks one egg at a time with a spatula.

Cut the Snickers into pieces and spread them over the bottom of the pie shell along with the peanuts. Pour the cheesecake mixture on top and smooth with a spatula. Bake in the middle of oven for 10 minutes. Reduce heat to 200 degrees Fahrenheit (105 degrees Celsius) and bake for 35 minutes (do not open oven door). Turn off the oven and let the cheesecake stand in the heat for another 25 minutes (which reduces the risk of cracking). Remove and let cool completely. Let the cheesecake stand in the fridge for at least 6 hours, preferably overnight, so that it hardens properly. Run a thin knife around the form's edge before it is removed. Rinse the knife with hot water a few times during that process.

FROSTING

Mix all the ingredients except the cream in a bowl and whisk until the mixture feels fluffy. Whip in the cream in batches until it becomes a smooth frosting. Pipe or spread the frosting over the cheesecake. Garnish with Snickers chunks and peanuts and, if you like, dust with cocoa powder.

12 slices

PIE SHELL

15 (200 g) graham crackers
⅓ cup + 1 tbsp (100 g) butter
¼ cup (40 g) sugar
1½ tbsp (10 g) cocoa powder
½ tsp (3 g) salt

CHEESECAKE FILLING

½ tsp vanilla extract
2½ cups (600 g) cream cheese
¾ cup (180 g) sugar
2 tbsp (20 g) all-purpose flour
¼ cup (59 mL (50 g)) whipping cream
2 (30 g) egg yolks
2 (110 g) eggs
1½ (80 g) Snickers bars
½ cup (60 g) salted peanuts

FROSTING

1¼ cups (300 g) cream cheese
2 tbsp (15 g) cocoa powder
¾ cups (120 g) powdered sugar
½ tsp (1½ g) vanilla extract
¼ cup (50 g) whipping cream

GARNISH

Pieces of Snickers
Salted peanuts
Optional, cocoa powder for dusting

PECAN TARTS

These small pies have a chewy and caramel-flavored filling with a nutty crunch. If you like pecans, this is the pie for you.

PIE SHELLS

Mix all the ingredients in a bowl or in a food processor and mix to a smooth dough. Wrap the dough in plastic and let it rest in the fridge for 20 minutes.

Roll the dough out on a floured work surface to a ¼ inch (3 mm) thick disk. Line eight pie forms with detachable edges, 3 inches (8 cm) in diameter, with the dough. Line up to the top edges and trim the excess dough with a knife. Prick the bottoms with a fork and let the shells stand in the freezer for 30 minutes. During this time, preheat the oven to 350 degrees Fahrenheit (180 degrees Celsius), convection function.

Bake pastry shells in the middle of the oven for 10 minutes and let them cool completely.

PECAN FILLING

Preheat the oven to 350 degrees Fahrenheit (170 degrees Celsius), convection function. Coarsely chop the pecan nuts. Melt the butter in a saucepan. Beat the eggs until fluffy in a bowl and then whisk in the melted butter. Then whisk in the brown sugar, sugar, flour, and vanilla extract. Finally, fold in the milk and nuts.

Divide the filling into the pastry shells and bake in the middle of oven about 15 minutes or until the surface has a nice golden brown color. Allow the pies to cool and then remove them carefully from the molds. Serve with lightly whipped cream.

8 portions of pie

PIE SHELLS

½ cup + 1 tsp (120 g) room temperature salted butter
½ cup (60 g) powdered sugar
1¼ cups (180 g) all-purpose flour
1 (15 g) egg yolk

PECAN FILLING

1 cup (150 g) pecans
½ cup (115 g) salted butter
2 (110 g) eggs
¾ cup (140 g) brown sugar
¼ cup (45 g) sugar
1 tbsp (9 g) all-purpose flour
1 tsp (3 g) vanilla extract
1 tbsp (15 mL (15 g)) milk

1⅔ cups (392 mL (400 g)) whipping cream for serving

APPLE CHEESECAKE

A creamy cheesecake with crunchy topping and rich flavors of apple, cinnamon, and vanilla. "Amazing," as most would agree.

PIE BOTTOM

Preheat the oven to 350 degrees Fahrenheit (180 degrees Celsius), convection function. Mix all the ingredients in a bowl or food processor and work together into a crumbly dough. Spread the dough evenly onto the bottom of a springform pan, 8½ inches (22 cm) in diameter. Flatten the surface lightly with the back of a tablespoon. Bake in the oven for 12 minutes. Allow to cool completely

CRUMBLE TOPPING

Mix all the ingredients in a bowl and pinch together to form a crumble.

CHEESECAKE FILLING

Preheat the oven to 325 degrees Fahrenheit (160 degrees Celsius), convection function. Mix 1 tablespoon of sugar, cinnamon, and nutmeg in a bowl. Peel, core, and cut the apples into pieces. Set the apple pieces in the bowl and mix well.

Beat the cream cheese, ¾ cup of sugar, vanilla extract, and flour into a fluffy mixture. Whisk in the cream. Fold in one egg at a time with a spatula.

Grease the mold's edges lightly with butter and pour in the filling. Sprinkle with apple pieces and distribute the crumble on top.

Bake in the oven for about 45 minutes or until the topping has browned slightly. Turn off the oven, crack open the door, and let the cheesecake stand in the heat for another 20 minutes. Remove and let cool completely. Then let the cheesecake stand in the refrigerator at least 6 hours, preferably overnight.

Run a thin knife around the edge of the mold before it is removed. Rinse the knife with hot water a few times during that process. Serve with caramelized milk as smooth as finished caramel sauce in a jar.

12 slices

PIE BOTTOM

½ cup (110 g) room temperature salted butter
¼ cup (45 g) sugar
1 cup (160 g) all-purpose flour

CRUMBLE TOPPING

¼ cup (50 g) sugar
⅔ cup (90 g) all-purpose flour
¼ cup (20 g) oats
¼ cup (60 g) room temperature salted butter
1 tsp (2 g) ground cardamom

CHEESECAKE FILLING

1 tbsp (14 g) sugar
1½ tsp (3 g) ground cinnamon
1 pinch ground nutmeg
2 large Granny Smith apples
2½ cups (600 g) cream cheese
¾ cup (180 g) sugar
½ tsp (2½ g) vanilla extract
2 tbsp (20 g) all-purpose flour
¼ cup (59 mL (50 g)) whipping cream
3 (165 g) eggs

CARAMEL SAUCE

1 can (ca 400 g) dulce de leche sauce

FROZEN PEANUT BUTTER CREAM PIE

This pie could probably work as a pre-marathon carbo-load because it contains just about all the energy you could need. Or you could do what I do and eat it anyway—because it's so damn good!

PIE SHELL

Preheat the oven to 350 degrees Fahrenheit (180 degrees Celsius), convection function. Scrape off the filling in the Oreo cookies and then run the biscuits into crumbs in a food processor. Melt the butter and add it to the crumbs. Blend thoroughly and line the inside of a spring or pie tin with a detachable edge, 8½ inches in diameter (22 cm), with the mixture. Flatten the surface lightly with the back of a tablespoon. Bake in the oven for about 10 minutes. Allow to cool.

DARK CHOCOLATE TRUFFLE

Chop the chocolate and place in a bowl. Bring the cream to a boil and pour it over the chocolate. Let stand for one minute and then fold with a spatula into a smooth truffle. Pour into the pie shell, sprinkle with peanuts, and leave in the freezer until the truffle has set. This takes about 40 minutes.

PEANUT FILLING

Whip the cream cheese, ¼ cup of cream, peanut butter, brown sugar, and vanilla extract until fluffy. Add 1 cup of cream in batches and whisk until the filling feels creamy and firm. Divide the filling evenly into the pie shell and let the pie stand in the freezer for at least 6 hours.

Remove the pie 10 minutes before serving. Lightly whip the cream and spread it on top. Finish by sprinkling with peanut butter cups and peanuts.

12 slices

PIE SHELL
25 (250 g) Oreo cookies
¼ cup (60 g) butter

DARK CHOCOLATE TRUFFLE
1 cup (150 g) dark chocolate
⅔ cup (157 mL (150 g)) whipping cream
½ cup (60 g) salted peanuts

PEANUT FILLING
1¾ cups (400 g) cream cheese
¼ cup (50 g) whipping cream
1 cup (350 g) smooth peanut butter
½ cup (100 g) brown sugar
½ tbsp (4 g) vanilla extract
1 cup (237 mL (250 g)) whipping cream

GARNISH
1¼ cups (295 mL (300 g)) whipping cream
6 Reese's Peanut Butter Cups, in bits
¼ cup (30 g) salted or natural peanuts

CHOCOLATE CHEESECAKE

I learned how to bake cheesecake from a real cheesecake queen in the United States. Making a creamy and delicious cheesecake requires patience while it's in the oven.

PIE BOTTOM

Preheat the oven to 350 degrees Fahrenheit (180 degrees Celsius), convection function. Scrape off the filling in the Oreo cookies and then run the biscuits to fine crumbs in a food processor. Melt the butter and add it to the crumbs. Mix well and then line the bottom of a springform, 9½ inches (24 cm) in diameter, with the mixture. Flatten the surface lightly with the back of a tablespoon. Bake in the middle of the oven for 10 minutes. Allow to cool completely.

CHEESECAKE FILLING

Preheat the oven to 400 degrees Fahrenheit (200 degrees Celsius), convection function. Chop and melt the chocolate gently in a water bath or microwave. Let cool to a lukewarm temperature. Beat the cream cheese, sugar, and salt with an electric mixer in a bowl until fluffy. Whisk in the sour cream. Fold in one egg at a time and the yolk with a spatula. Finally, carefully fold in the chocolate.

Pour the filling into the mold, smooth the surface with a spatula, and bake in middle of the oven for 10 minutes. Reduce heat to 225 degrees Fahrenheit (110 degrees Celsius) (do not open oven door) and bake for 60 minutes. Turn off the oven and let the cheesecake stand in the residual heat for another 40 minutes. Remove and let cool.

Let the cheesecake stand in the fridge for at least 6 hours, preferably overnight, so that it hardens properly.

Run a thin knife around the edge of the mold before it is removed. Rinse the knife with hot water a few times during that process. Spread whipped cream on top and drizzle the melted chocolate. Finish by sprinkling the shaved chocolate over the pie.

12 slices

PIE BOTTOM

20 (200 g) Oreo cookies
¼ cup (50 g) unsalted butter

CHEESECAKE FILLING

1¾ cups (250 g) dark chocolate, 70%
3¾ cups (900 g) room temperature cream cheese
1⅓ cups (300 g) sugar
½ tsp (3 g) salt
¾ cup (200 g) room temperature sour cream
3 (165 g) eggs, room temperature
1 (15 g) egg yolk

GARNISH

1¼ cups (295 mL (300 g)) whipping cream
¼ cup (50 g) melted dark chocolate, 70%
¼ cup (50 g) shaved dark chocolate, 70%

STRAWBERRY CHEESECAKE

This is a real New York Cheesecake. Tall, creamy, silky smooth, and truly, truly lovely.

PIE BOTTOM

Preheat the oven to 350 degrees Fahrenheit (180 degrees Celsius), convection function. Run the crackers into fine crumbs in a food processor. Add the sugar and mix together. Melt the butter and add it. Mix well and distribute the mixture evenly on the bottom of a springform, 8½ inches (22 cm) in diameter. Flatten the surface lightly with the back of a tablespoon. Bake in the oven for 10 minutes. Allow to cool completely.

CHEESECAKE FILLING

Preheat the oven to 400 degrees Fahrenheit (200 degrees Celsius), convection function. Beat the cream cheese and sugar in a bowl until fluffy. Add the vanilla extract, and mix them in the bowl together with the flour. Whisk for 3–4 minutes and then fold in the sour cream with a spatula. Then fold in one egg at a time and the egg yolk and mix thoroughly.

Pour batter into pan and bake in middle of oven for 10 minutes. Reduce heat to 225 degrees Fahrenheit (110 degrees Celsius) (do not open the door) and bake for 55 minutes. Turn off the oven and let the cheesecake stand in the residual heat for another 50 minutes. Remove and let cool. Let the cheesecake stand in the fridge for at least 6 hours, preferably overnight, so that it hardens properly.

STRAWBERRY SAUCE

Boil the strawberries, sugar, and lime juice until the strawberries have become mushy. Blend the mixture until smooth with a hand blender and pass the sauce through a sieve. Allow to cool in the fridge.

Draw a thin knife around the edge of the mold before it is removed. Rinse the knife with hot water a few times during that process. Drizzle the strawberry sauce over the pie and garnish with strawberries.

12 slices

PIE BOTTOM

15 (200 g) graham crackers
2 tbsp (28 g) sugar
⅓ cup + 1 tbsp (100 g) salted butter

CHEESECAKE FILLING

3¾ cups (900 g) cream cheese
1¼ cups (255 g) sugar
½ tsp vanilla extract
¼ cup (30 g) all-purpose flour
1 cup (250 g) sour cream
3 (165 g) eggs
1 (15 g) egg yolk

STRAWBERRY SAUCE

1 lbs (500 g) strawberries (frozen or fresh)
½ cup (90 g) sugar
Juice from one lime

20 fresh strawberries for decorating

CUPCAKES
and
CAKE POPS

BEV

Beverly Hills is a small city in Los Angeles County. It's probably no exaggeration to call Beverly Hills the epicenter of the celebrity world. Here you'll find some of the most expensive homes in the United States, as well as the legendary shopping street—**Rodeo Drive**—with its famous designer stores, such as Gucci, Chanel, Prada and Versace.

When I am in Beverly Hills, I sometimes feel as if I'm walking around in a movie—it's so unreal and almost perfect. Everything is beautiful and everyone is beautiful. A little too much of everything. But I like it! On expensive Rodeo Drive, people are both dressed-up and made-up to the max. And if you're lucky, you might spot a celebrity. But it's not all about brands and celebrities here. There are also many good restaurants and bakeries, and in the latter category I have two favorites—**Crumbs Bake Shop** (9465 Little Santa Monica Boulevard) and **Sprinkles Cupcakes** (9635 South Santa Monica Boulevard). If you're ever in Beverly Hills, be sure to visit them!

ERLY HILLS

CAPPUCCINO CUPCAKES

With all due respect to piping and decorating, why not try something playful and serve your cupcakes in a cup? Bake as usual, and then move into cups. A little cappuccino frosting and powdered cacao on top, and now the perfect coffee break can begin!

CUPCAKE BATTER

Preheat the oven to 350 degrees Fahrenheit (170 degrees Celsius), convection function. Sift the dry ingredients into a mixing bowl. Whisk together the eggs, vanilla extract, milk, and oil lightly in another bowl. Fold in the dry ingredients with a spatula. Add the hot coffee a little at a time and mix until it becomes a smooth batter.

Place the cupcake wrappers in a cupcake pan or use two wrappers at a time on a regular sheet. Fill the wrappers three-quarters with the batter and bake in the middle of the oven for about 18 minutes. Use a toothpick to test that the cupcakes are baked through. Let cool completely and then, optionally, transfer the cupcakes to cups.

CAPPUCCINO FROSTING

Beat the cream cheese and butter in a bowl until fluffy. Add the powdered sugar and beat on maximum speed until it becomes a nice and creamy frosting. Finally, mix in the coffee thoroughly.

Generously pipe frosting on each cupcake and finish by dusting with a little cacao.

12 cupcakes

CUPCAKE BATTER

¾ cup (120 g) all-purpose flour
½ cup (40 g) cocoa powder
¾ cup (180 g) sugar
½ tsp (2 g) baking powder
½ tsp (2 g) baking soda
½ tsp (3 g) salt
1 (55 g) egg
⅓ cup (79 mL (75 g)) whole milk
½ tsp (1½ g) vanilla extract
¼ cup (59 mL (45 g)) vegetable oil
¼ cup (59 mL (50 g)) warm espresso coffee

CAPPUCCINO FROSTING

1¼ cups (300 g) cream cheese
½ cup (100 g) room temperature salted butter
1⅔ cups (240 g) powdered sugar
2 tbsp (30 mL (30 g)) cooled espresso coffee

Cacao for dusting

NUTELLA CUPCAKES

This is absolutely one of my best cupcake recipes. You'll need a star-shaped piping tip for this particular frosting. Pipe by moving your way from the inside out. That way the frosting will have this lovely rose pattern. Simple but impressive!

CUPCAKE BATTER

Preheat the oven to 350 degrees Fahrenheit (170 degrees Celsius), convection function. Sift the dry ingredients into a bowl. Whisk together the eggs, vanilla extract, milk, and oil lightly in another bowl. Fold in the dry ingredients with a spatula. Add the coffee little by little and mix until it becomes a thin and smooth batter.

Place the cupcake wrappers in a cupcake pan or use two wrappers at a time on a regular sheet. Fill the wrappers three-quarters with the batter and bake in the middle of the oven for about 16–17 minutes. Use a toothpick to test that the cupcakes are baked through. Let cool completely.

NUTELLA FROSTING

Chop the chocolate and melt it gently in a water bath or in the microwave. Allow to cool to lukewarm temperature. Beat the butter, powdered sugar, vanilla extract, and salt in a bowl until fluffy. Add the Nutella and chocolate and whisk thoroughly. If the frosting seems too loose, it can be set in the fridge for 10 minutes to solidify a bit. Pipe frosting on each cupcake and decorate with sprinkles if you like.

12 cupcakes

CUPCAKE BATTER

¾ cup (100 g) all-purpose flour
¾ cup (150 g) sugar
⅓ cup (30 g) cocoa powder
½ tsp (3 g) baking powder
½ tsp (3 g) baking soda
1 tsp (3 g) corn starch
½ tsp (3 g) salt
1 (55 g) egg
⅓ cup (79 mL (75 g)) whole milk
½ tbsp (5 g) vanilla extract
¼ cup (59 mL (45 g)) vegetable oil
¼ cup (59 mL (50 g)) warm coffee or boiling water

NUTELLA FROSTING

1 cup (150 g) dark chocolate, 70%
1 cup + 2 tbsp (250 g) room temperature salted butter
1 cup (150 g) powdered sugar
½ tbsp (5 g) vanilla extract
¼ tsp (2 g) salt
⅓ cup (100 g) Nutella

Optional: chocolate sprinkles for garnish

CHOCOLATE RASPBERRY CUPCAKES

Cupcakes that will make your guests say, "Wow!" They're moist and chocolaty with a wonderfully fluffy meringue buttercream topping. They are pure happiness— both to look at and to eat.

CUPCAKE BATTER

Preheat the oven to 350 degrees Fahrenheit (170 degrees Celsius), convection function. Sift the dry ingredients into a bowl. Whisk together the eggs, vanilla extract, and oil lightly in another bowl. Fold in the dry ingredients with a spatula. Add the water little by little and mix until it becomes a thin and smooth batter.

Place the cupcake wrappers in a cupcake pan or use two wrappers at a time on a regular sheet. Fill the wrappers three-quarters with the batter and bake in the middle of the oven for about 16–17 minutes. Use a toothpick to test that the cupcakes are baked through. Let cool completely.

MERINGUE BUTTERCREAM

Pass the raspberries through a sieve to achieve a smooth purée. Beat the egg whites and sugar by hand in a water bath until the sugar has dissolved. Remove the bowl from the heat and continue to whip, now with an electric blender until the meringue is stiff and cool. Add the vanilla extract and any food coloring. Whisk in the butter in batches until it becomes a nice and smooth cream. Add the raspberry purée in batches and mix well.

CHOCOLATE SAUCE

Chop the chocolate and place in a bowl. Bring the cream to a boil and pour it into the bowl. Let stand for one minute and stir, then combine into a smooth sauce. Allow to cool completely.

Generously pipe meringue buttercream on each cupcake and top with chocolate sauce and fresh raspberries.

15 cupcakes

CUPCAKE BATTER

¾ cup (120 g) all-purpose flour
¾ cup (190 g) sugar
½ tsp (3 g) baking powder
1 tsp (5 g) baking soda
½ tsp (3 g) salt
⅔ cup (60 g) cocoa powder
1 (55 g) egg
½ tsp (1½ g) vanilla extract
⅔ cup (157 mL (120 g)) vegetable oil
1 cup (237 mL (225 g)) hot water

MERINGUE BUTTERCREAM

½ lb (200 g) raspberries
4 (150 g) egg whites
1¼ cups (255 g) sugar
¾ tbsp (7½ g) vanilla extract
Optional: red food coloring
1½ cups + 2 tsp (350 g) room temperature unsalted butter

CHOCOLATE SAUCE

¾ cup (100 g) dark chocolate, 70%
½ cup (118 mL (100 g)) whipping cream

Fresh raspberries for topping

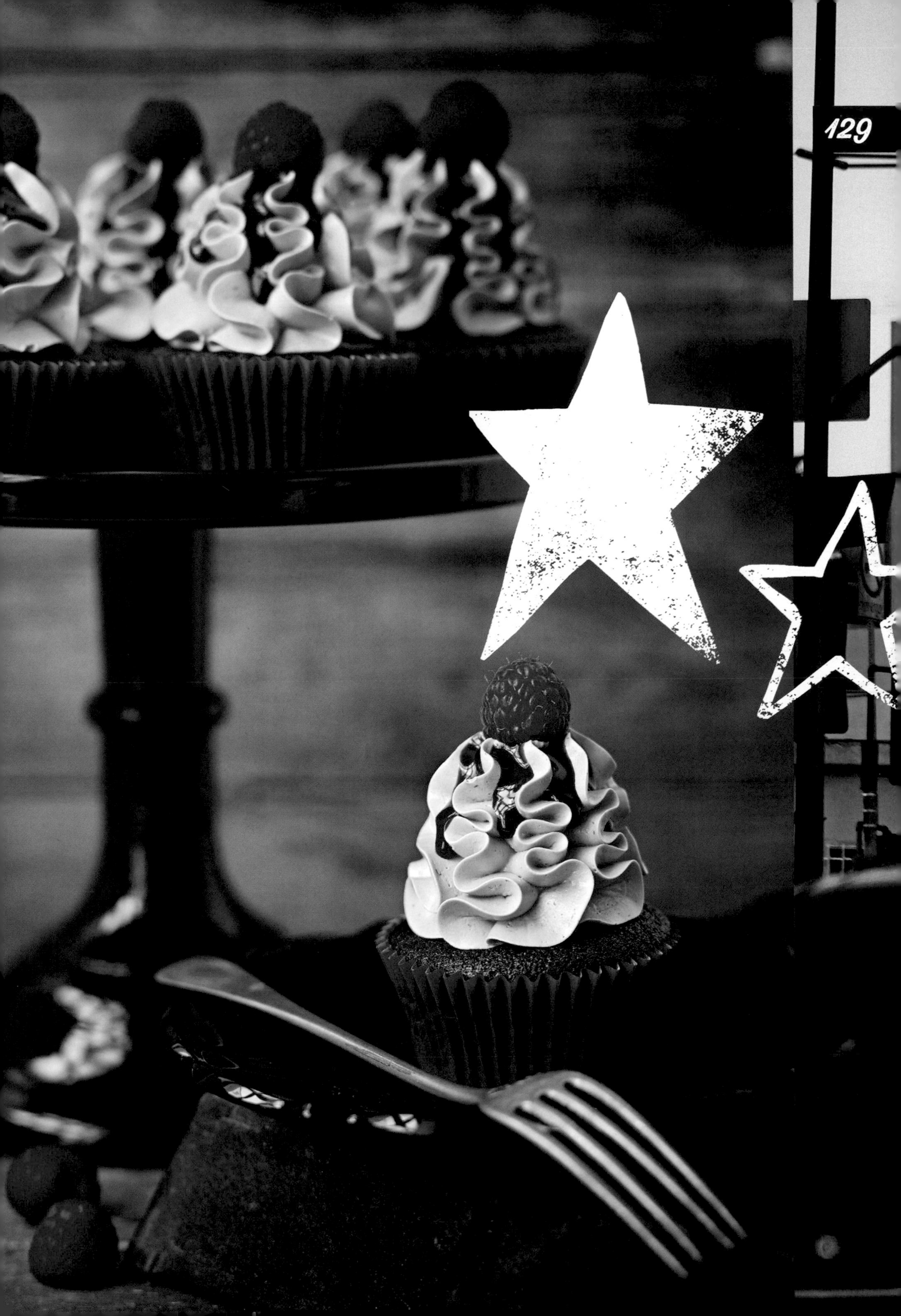

COCONUT CUPCAKES

Say "Aloha!" to the ultimate coconut cupcake. If you're thinking of a moist coconut macaroon with a soft and creamy coconut topping, then you just about understand the voluptuous taste that awaits you!

CUPCAKE BATTER

Preheat the oven to 325 degrees Fahrenheit (160 degrees Celsius), convection function. Mix together the milk and vinegar in a small bowl. Sift the dry ingredients in a bowl. Beat the butter, vanilla extract, and sugar until fluffy in a separate bowl. Mix in the eggs one at a time into butter mixture. Stir in the dry ingredients and milk mixture in batches. Add the coconut and mix until it becomes smooth.

Place the cupcake wrappers in a cupcake pan or use two wrappers at a time on a regular sheet. Fill the wrappers three-quarters with the batter and bake in the middle of the oven for about 20 minutes. Use a toothpick to test that the cupcakes are baked-through. Let cool completely.

FROSTING

Beat the cream cheese and butter in a bowl until fluffy. Add the powdered sugar and vanilla extract and whisk on maximum speed until it has become a nice and creamy frosting. Optionally, mix in the liqueur.

Pipe a ball of frosting on each cupcake and sprinkle with coconut.

13 cupcakes

CUPCAKE BATTER

⅔ cup (157 mL (125 g)) whole milk
1 tsp (5 mL (5 g)) white distilled vinegar
1¼ cups (180 g) all-purpose flour
½ tsp (3 g) salt
½ tsp (3 g) baking powder
¼ tsp (2 g) baking soda
¾ cup (170 g) room temperature unsalted butter
¼ tbsp (2 g) vanilla extract
¾ cup (180 g) sugar
3 (165 g) eggs
½ lb (200 g) shredded coconut

FROSTING

1¼ cups (300 g) cream cheese
¼ cup (50 g) room temperature unsalted butter
1⅔ cups (240 g) powdered sugar
½ tbsp (5 g) vanilla extract

Optional: 2 tbsp (30 mL (20 g)) Malibu liqueur
¼ lb (100 g) shaved coconut for sprinkling

LEMON MERINGUE CUPCAKES

Because I love lemon meringue pie, I wanted to create a cupcake that was just like it. These are light and airy cupcakes. There's a strong chance you'll sneak two, if not more!

LEMON CURD

Boil the lemon juice and sugar in a saucepan. Lower the heat. Add the egg and egg yolk and heat while stirring constantly until the cream begins to thicken. Pass the cream through a strainer into a bowl and add the butter. Stir until the butter melts. Let stand in refrigerator for 1 hour.

CUPCAKE BATTER

Preheat the oven to 350 degrees Fahrenheit (170 degrees Celsius), convection function. Mix together the milk and vinegar in a bowl. Beat the butter, vanilla extract, and sugar in a bowl until fluffy. Sift the dry ingredients in another bowl. Mix in the eggs one at a time and the yolk into butter mixture. Stir in the dry ingredients and milk mixture in batches and mix until it becomes a smooth batter. Add the lemon juice and zest and mix well.

Place the cupcake wrappers in a cupcake pan or use two wrappers at a time on a regular sheet. Fill the wrappers three-quarters with the batter and bake in the middle of the oven for about 18 minutes. Use a toothpick to test that the cupcakes are baked through. Let cool completely.

ITALIAN MERINGUE

Beat the egg whites in a bowl until stiff. Carefully boil the water and sugar to 250 degrees Fahrenheit (121 degrees Celsius). Check the temperature with a candy thermometer. Pour the syrup in the bowl immediately in a thin stream down into the bowl and whisk together with an electric whisk on maximum speed. Whisk on medium speed until the meringue is cool.

Scoop out a hole in each cupcake and fill with lemon curd. Pipe the meringue and brulee it with a torch.

15 cupcakes

LEMON CURD
⅓ cup (79 mL (75 g)) freshly squeezed lemon juice
½ cup (90 g) sugar
1 (55 g) egg
1 (15 g) egg yolk
¼ cup (50 g) unsalted butter

CUPCAKE BATTER
1 cup (237 mL (250 g)) whole milk
1 tbsp (15 mL (10 g)) white distilled vinegar
½ cup + 1 tsp (120 g) room temperature salted butter
1¼ cups (250 g) sugar
1⅔ cups (240 g) all-purpose flour
1½ tsp (8 g) baking powder
½ tsp (2 g) baking soda
½ tsp (3 g) salt
2 (110 g) eggs
½ tbsp (4 g) vanilla extract
1 (15 g) egg yolk
¼ cup (59 mL (50 g)) freshly squeezed lemon juice + grated zest from 2 lemons

ITALIAN MERINGUE
4 (125 g) egg whites
⅓ cup (75 g) water
1 cup (210 g) sugar

OREO CUPCAKES

Oreo cookies have been around for over a hundred years, and they are probably the best-selling cookie in the United States. It's easy to see why. This is a slightly different recipe, for at the bottom of every cupcake lies an Oreo cookie—baked in like a little surprise.

CUPCAKE BATTER

Preheat the oven to 350 degrees Fahrenheit (170 degrees Celsius), convection function. Place the cupcake wrappers in a cupcake pan or use two wrappers at a time on a regular sheet. Place an Oreo cookie in each form.

Sift the dry ingredients in a bowl. Whisk together eggs, milk, vanilla extract, and oil lightly in another bowl.

Fold in the dry ingredients with a spatula. Add the boiling hot water a little at a time and mix until it becomes smooth.

Fill the wrappers just about three-quarters with the batter and bake in the middle of the oven for about 15 minutes. Use a toothpick to test that the cupcakes are baked through. Let cool completely.

OREO FROSTING

Scrape off the filling of the Oreo cookies and then run the cookies to fine crumbs in a food processor. Whisk together the butter and cream cheese with electric mixer in a bowl, scraping the sides with a spatula in between. Add the powdered sugar and vanilla extract and whisk for a minute at low speed. Whisk on maximum speed until the frosting feels nice and solid. Fold in the cookie crumbs with a spatula and mix well.

Pipe frosting on each cupcake. Halve the Oreo cookies for decoration and press one half into the frosting on each cupcake.

14 cupcakes

CUPCAKE BATTER

14 (140 g) Oreo cookies
¾ cup (120 g) all-purpose flour
¾ cup (150 g) sugar
⅓ cup (30 g) cocoa powder
½ tsp (3 g) baking powder
½ tsp (3 g) baking soda
½ tsp (3 g) salt
1 (55 g) egg
⅓ cup (79 mL (75 g)) whole milk
½ tbsp (5g) vanilla extract
¼ cup (59 mL (45 g)) vegetable oil
¼ cup (59 mL (50 g)) boiling hot water

OREO FROSTING

5 cookies (50 g) Oreo cookies + 7 cookies (70 g) for decoration
¼ cup (50 g) room temperature unsalted butter
1¼ cups (300 g) cream cheese
1⅔ cups (240 g) powdered sugar
¼ tbsp (2½ g) vanilla extract

S'MORES!

» I've always wondered why these little delights were called s 'mores. On this trip, I finally learned the answer: children, who tried these treats of grilled marshmallows, sandwiched between two crackers and a chocolate bar found them to be so incredibly delicious that they cried out for more. "Some more" sounds a bit like s' more if you say it quickly. And I can promise you that you'll want some more. Right away!

S'MORES CUPCAKES

After trying grilled s'mores (see the previous pages) and falling completely in love with them, I wanted to make a cupcake that matched the experience. A graham cracker bottom covered with chocolate and marshmallow. A cupcake over that and on top a fluffy Italian meringue that melts in your mouth. I can guarantee that everyone will want more!

BOTTOMS

Preheat the oven to 350 degrees Fahrenheit (170 degrees Celsius), convection function. Place the cupcake wrappers in a cupcake pan or use two wrappers at a time on a regular sheet. Melt the butter in a saucepan. Crumble the graham crackers and place the crumbs in a bowl. Add the sugar and butter and mix. Distribute the crumble mixture in the molds and smooth the surface with the back of a spoon. Bake in the middle of the oven for four minutes. Remove the sheet from the oven and sprinkle with shaved chocolate in every form. Add four mini marshmallows to each one once the chocolate has melted.

CUPCAKE BATTER

Sift the dry ingredients in a bowl. Whisk together the eggs, milk, vanilla extract, and oil lightly in another bowl. Fold in the dry ingredients with a spatula and mix until it becomes smooth. Fill the molds just about three-quarters with batter and bake in the middle of the oven for about 15 minutes. Allow to cool completely.

ITALIAN MERINGUE

Beat the egg whites until stiff in a bowl. Carefully boil the water and sugar to 350 degrees Fahrenheit (170 degrees Celsius). Check the temperature with a candy thermometer. Immediately pour the syrup in a thin stream down into the bowl and whisk together with mixer at maximum speed. Then beat at medium speed until the meringue is cold. Pipe or spread the meringue on each cupcake and brûlée it with a torch.

12 cupcakes

BOTTOMS

¼ cup (50 g) butter
8 (100 g) graham crackers
1 tbsp (15 g) sugar
¾ cup (100 g) shaved dark
   chocolate
48 mini marshmallows

CUPCAKE BATTER

1 cup (140 g) all-purpose
   flour
¾ cup (170 g) sugar
½ cup (45 g) cocoa powder
½ tsp (2 g) baking powder
½ tsp (2 g) baking soda
½ tsp (3 g) salt
1 (55 g) egg
½ tsp (1½ g) vanilla extract
¾ cup (177 mL (125 g))
   whole milk
¼ cup (59 mL (45 g))
   vegetable oil

ITALIAN MERINGUE

4 (125 g) egg whites
⅓ cup (79 mL (75 g)) water
1 cup (210 g) sugar

SNICKERDOODLE CUPCAKES

I decided on the name "snickerdoodle" because I thought it sounded so fun. Snickerdoodle is a good, rustic cookie flavored with cinnamon. My cupcakes have the same flavor but with icing on top. These cupcakes go well with any occasion—especially the Christmas season.

CUPCAKE BATTER

Preheat the oven to 350 degrees Fahrenheit (170 degrees Celsius), convection function. Place the cupcake wrappers in a cupcake pan or use two wrappers at a time on a regular sheet.

Mix the dry ingredients in a stand mixer using the beater blade attachment, or use an electric beater and bowl. Add the butter and mix for a minute. Stir in the sour cream, vanilla extract, and eggs and work together to make a smooth and fine batter.

Fill the wrappers just about three-quarters with the batter and bake in the middle of the oven for about 18 minutes. Use a toothpick to test that the cupcakes are baked through. Let cool completely.

FROSTING

Whisk together the butter and cream cheese with electric mixer in a bowl, scraping the sides with a spatula in between. Add the powdered sugar, vanilla extract, and cinnamon and whisk for a minute on low speed. Then whisk again at maximum speed until the frosting feels nice and solid. Pipe frosting on each cupcake and sprinkle sugar and cinnamon over them.

12 cupcakes

CUPCAKE BATTER

1¼ cups (180 g) all-purpose flour
¾ cups (180 g) sugar
1½ tsp (7 g) baking powder
1½ tsp (3 g) ground cinnamon
½ tsp (1 g) ground nutmeg
½ tsp (3 g) salt
½ cup + 1 tsp (120 g) room temperature unsalted butter
½ cup (100 g) sour cream
2 (110 g) eggs, room temperature
½ tsp (1½ g) vanilla extract

FROSTING

¼ cup (60 g) room temperature unsalted butter
¾ cup (200 g) cream cheese
2½ cups (360 g) powdered sugar
½ tbsp (5 g) vanilla extract
1 tsp (2 g) ground cinnamon

Sugar and ground cinnamon for sprinkling

PEANUT BUTTER CUPCAKES

Americans probably consume the most peanut butter of any country in the world. It's in almost everything! In sandwiches, ice cream, pancakes, cupcakes, cakes, cookies, you name it! It's also in candy, of course, just like the decoration I used on these cupcakes. Reese's Peanut Butter Cups can be found in the candy aisle of any grocery store, convenience store, or drug store. If not, use peanuts.

CUPCAKE BATTER

Preheat the oven to 350 degrees Fahrenheit (170 degrees Celsius), convection function. Combine the milk and vinegar in a bowl. Sift the flour, baking soda, baking powder, and salt in a bowl. Beat the brown sugar, butter, and peanut butter in another bowl until fluffy. Whisk the egg into the butter mixture. Stir in the dry ingredients and milk mixture in batches. Mix until it becomes smooth.

Place the cupcake wrappers in a cupcake pan or use two wrappers at a time on a regular sheet. Fill the wrappers just about three-quarters with the batter and bake in the middle of the oven for about 19 minutes. Use a toothpick to test that the cupcakes are baked through. Let cool completely.

PEANUT FROSTING

Whisk the peanut butter until fluffy with an electric beater in a bowl. Stir in the powdered sugar, vanilla extract, and salt. Add the cream in batches and whisk until it becomes a nice and solid frosting. Pipe frosting on each cupcake and garnish with peanut butter cups.

12 cupcakes

CUPCAKE BATTER

¾ cup (177 mL (175 g)) whole milk
½ tbsp (7½ mL (5 g)) white distilled vinegar
1 cup (150 g) all-purpose flour
½ tsp (3 g) baking soda
¼ tsp (2 g) baking powder
½ tsp (3 g) salt
¾ cup (150 g) brown sugar
¼ cup (50 g) room temperature unsalted butter
½ cup (150 g) crunchy peanut butter
1 (55 g) egg

PEANUT FROSTING

⅔ cup (200 g) smooth peanut butter
¼ cup + 1 tbsp (70 g) room temperature unsalted butter
¾ cup (120 g) powdered sugar
½ tbsp (5 g) vanilla extract
½ tsp (3 g) salt
¼ cup (59 mL (50 g)) whipping cream

12 halved Reese's Peanut Butter Cups for garnishing

BUSTED!

>> Regardless of your day job, everyone enjoys a good dessert break—especially if it involves cupcakes. Even the tough guys! When I offered cupcakes to this policeman, Byron Holloway, he was really excited because they're so incredibly good!

PEANUT BUTTER CAKE POPS

An ingenious person somewhere decided to put a mashed cupcake on a stick, dip it in chocolate, and finely decorate it. An idea that suits my style perfectly! Cake pops are so incredibly good and the ideal treat when you simply want something small with your coffee.

FILLING

Preheat the oven to 350 degrees Fahrenheit (170 degrees Celsius), convection function. Grease an oblong baking pan, 6 cups (1½ liters), and line the base with parchment paper.

Melt the butter in a saucepan. Sift the dry ingredients in a bowl. Beat the eggs and sugar until white and fluffy with an electric mixer in another bowl. Stir in the dry ingredients and then add the milk, vanilla extract, and butter in batches. Mix until it becomes a smooth batter, pour the batter in the form, and bake in the middle of the oven for about 35 minutes. Use a toothpick to test if it has been baked-through. Allow to cool.

Crumble the cake in a food processor. Add the peanut butter and cream cheese and mix together until it becomes a smooth and firm dough. Cover with plastic wrap and leave in the fridge for 30 minutes.

Roll into round balls of dough and place them on a tray covered with parchment paper or plastic wrap.

DIPPING AND DECORATION

Melt a bit of milk chocolate gently in a water bath or in the microwave. Dip the tip of a stick in the chocolate and then insert the stick into a dough ball. Stand or place back on the tray and repeat with the rest of the balls. Let cool in the fridge for 30 minutes.

Melt the rest of the chocolate. Dip each cake pop one at a time in the chocolate, allow the chocolate to run off, then roll in the chopped peanuts. Stick the pop in a piece of Styrofoam or something similar and let it set.

30 cake pops

FILLING
⅓ cup + 1 tbsp (100 g) salted butter
½ cup (45 g) cocoa powder
⅔ cup (90 g) all-purpose flour
½ tsp (3 g) baking powder
½ tsp (4 g) salt
3 (160 g) eggs
¾ cup (180 g) sugar
½ cup (118 mL (100 g)) whole milk
¼ tbsp (2½ g) vanilla extract
1¼ cups (350 g) crunchy peanut butter
¾ cup (200 g) cream cheese

DIPPING AND DECORATION
2¼ cups (300 g) milk chocolate
Finely-chopped, salted peanuts

30 cake pop sticks

OREO CAKE POPS

These small goodies are childishly good. But they are definitely not just for kids!

23 cake pops

OREO FILLING
50 (500 g) Oreo cookies
½ cup (150 g) cream cheese

DIPPING AND DECORATION
1¾ cups (300 g) white chocolate
5 (50 g) Oreo cookies

23 cake pop sticks

OREO FILLING
Turn all of the cookies to fine crumbs in food processor. Add cream cheese and process until it becomes a dough. Wrap the dough in plastic and leave it in the fridge for 30 minutes.

Roll the dough into round balls and place them on a tray covered with parchment paper or plastic wrap.

DIPPING AND DECORATION
Melt the white chocolate gently in a water bath or in a microwave. Dip the tip of a stick in the chocolate and then insert into a dough ball. Stand or place back on the tray and repeat the procedure with the rest of the balls. Allow to solidify in the refrigerator for 15 minutes.

Scrape off the filling from the Oreos. Then turn the cookies to fine crumbs in a food processor. Dip each cake pop one at a time in the chocolate, allow the chocolate to run off, then stick the pop in a piece of Styrofoam or something similar. Sprinkle with the Oreo crumbs and let the chocolate harden.

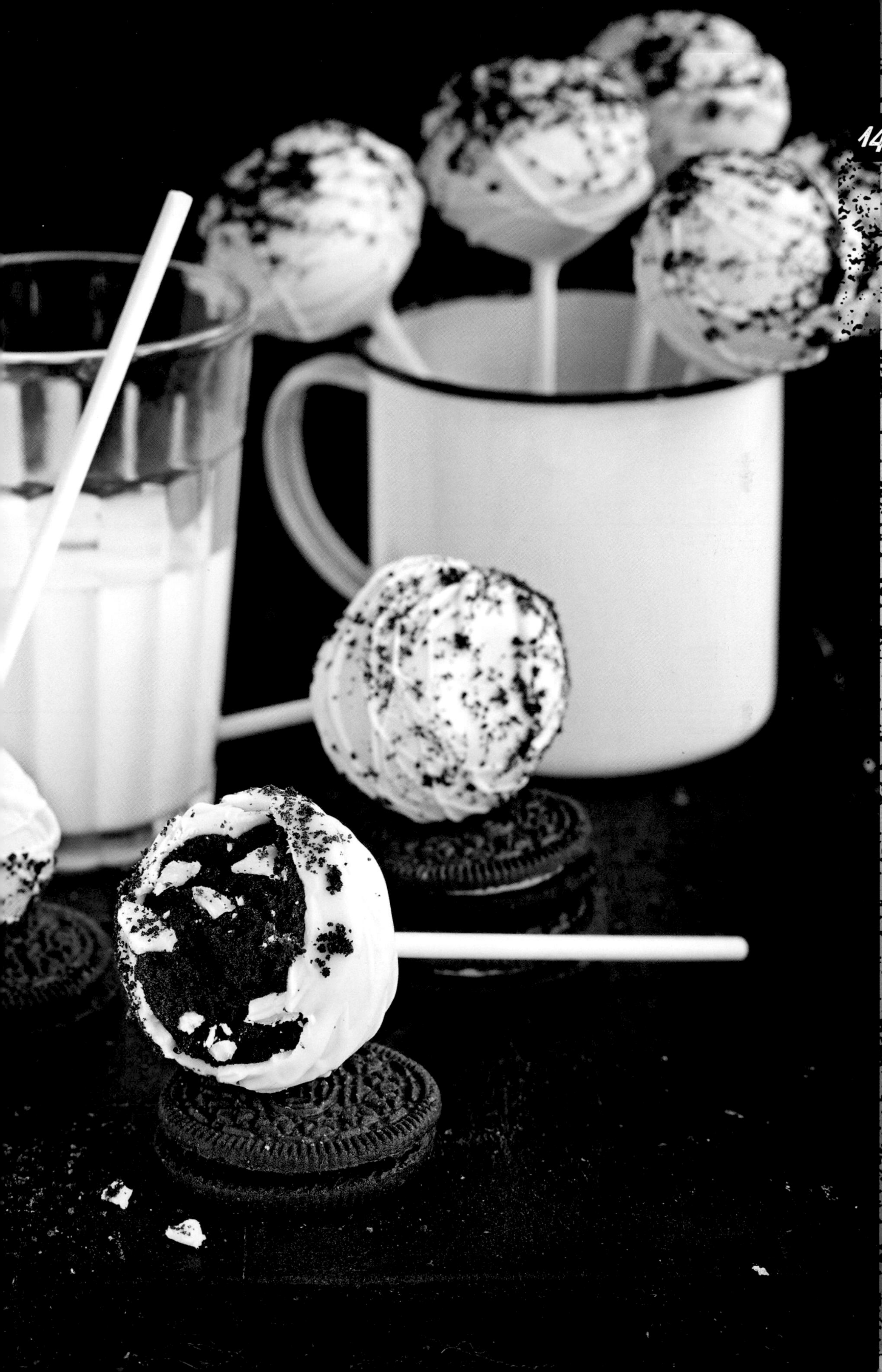

NUTELLA CAKE POPS

Nutella, like peanut butter, is a big favorite in the kitchen. With its smooth consistency and rich chocolate and hazelnut flavors, it goes with almost everything.

FILLING

Preheat the oven to 350 degrees Fahrenheit (175 degrees Celsius), convection function. Grease an oblong baking pan, 6 cups (1 ½ liters), and line the base with parchment paper.

Melt the butter in a saucepan. Sift the dry ingredients in a bowl. Beat the eggs, vanilla extract, and sugar until white and fluffy with electric mixer in another bowl. Stir in the dry ingredients and then add the milk and butter in batches. Mix until it becomes a smooth batter, pour the batter in the mold, and bake in the middle of the oven for about 35 minutes. Use a toothpick to be sure the cake is baked through. Allow to cool.

Crumble the chocolate cake in a food processor. Add the Nutella and mix together until a smooth and firm dough. Cover the dough with plastic wrap and leave in the fridge for 30 minutes.

Roll the dough into the round balls and place them on a tray covered with parchment paper or plastic wrap.

DIPPING AND DECORATION

Melt the dark chocolate gently in a water bath or in a microwave. Dip the tip of a stick in the chocolate and then insert into a dough ball. Stand or place back on the tray and repeat the procedure with the rest of the balls. Allow to solidify in the refrigerator for 15 minutes.

Dip each cake pop one at a time in the chocolate, allow the chocolate to run off, then stick the pop in a piece of Styrofoam or something similar. Let stand until the chocolate has hardened. Melt the milk chocolate gently in a water bath or in microwave and use it to decorate the cake pops.

25 cake pops

FILLING

⅓ cup + 1 tbsp (100 g) salted butter
½ cup (45 g) cocoa powder
⅔ cup (90 g) all-purpose flour
½ tsp (3 g) baking powder
½ tsp (4 g) salt
3 (160 g) eggs
¾ cup (180 g) sugar
½ cup (118 mL (100 g)) whole milk
¼ tbsp (2½ g) vanilla extract
½ cup (150 g) Nutella

DIPPING AND DECORATION

2¼ cups (300 g) dark chocolate, 70 %
¾ cup (100 g) milk chocolate

25 cake pop sticks

Sweet
BREAKFAST

GOOD

>> **Breakfast** often includes a little extra of everything and consists of many sweet dishes. Maybe not an option I would choose every morning, but there are certainly lots of goodies to enjoy! When I was in Los Angeles and working on the photos for this book, I wanted to invite my friends to a lovely, sweet breakfast. And to make it a little more fun, I made it into a picnic. We were in California, so you can always rely on the weather.

I chose my breakfast favorites—from pancakes and yogurt to cinnamon rolls and blueberry muffins.

With all the goodies in a basket and a big blanket, we went to a nice little park. Super Cozy!

A simpler version for sleepy-heads, of course, is to set a table with your treats in the kitchen, on the balcony, or in the garden. Then you can also treat yourself to a little extra with waffles. They're best freshly made.

MORNING

APPLE PANCAKES

It's important to cook the pancakes over medium heat so that the baking powder has time to work. Then they'll be nice and fluffy. Using a small pancake pan makes the results extra fine, but you can, of course, do just as well without one.

Approx. 7 pancakes

1⅔ cups (240 g) all-purpose flour
1½ tsp (7 g) baking powder
1½ tsp (3 g) ground cinnamon
¼ cup (50 g) sugar
½ tsp (2 g) salt
3 (160 g) eggs
1½ cups (355 mL (350 g)) whole milk
½ tsp (2 g) vanilla extract
3 apples
Butter for frying

FOR SERVING
Powdered sugar
Ground cinnamon
Maple syrup
Chopped nuts
1 pint (½ liter) vanilla ice cream

Sift the dry ingredients in a bowl. Whisk together the eggs, vanilla extract, and milk in another bowl. In batches whisk the dry ingredients into the egg mixture. Shred the apples and mix into the batter.

Cook the pancakes over low heat, preferably in a pan with a diameter of about 5 inches, with a little melted butter. Sprinkle icing sugar and cinnamon over the pancakes. Drizzle with maple syrup, sprinkle with chopped nuts, and serve with ice cream.

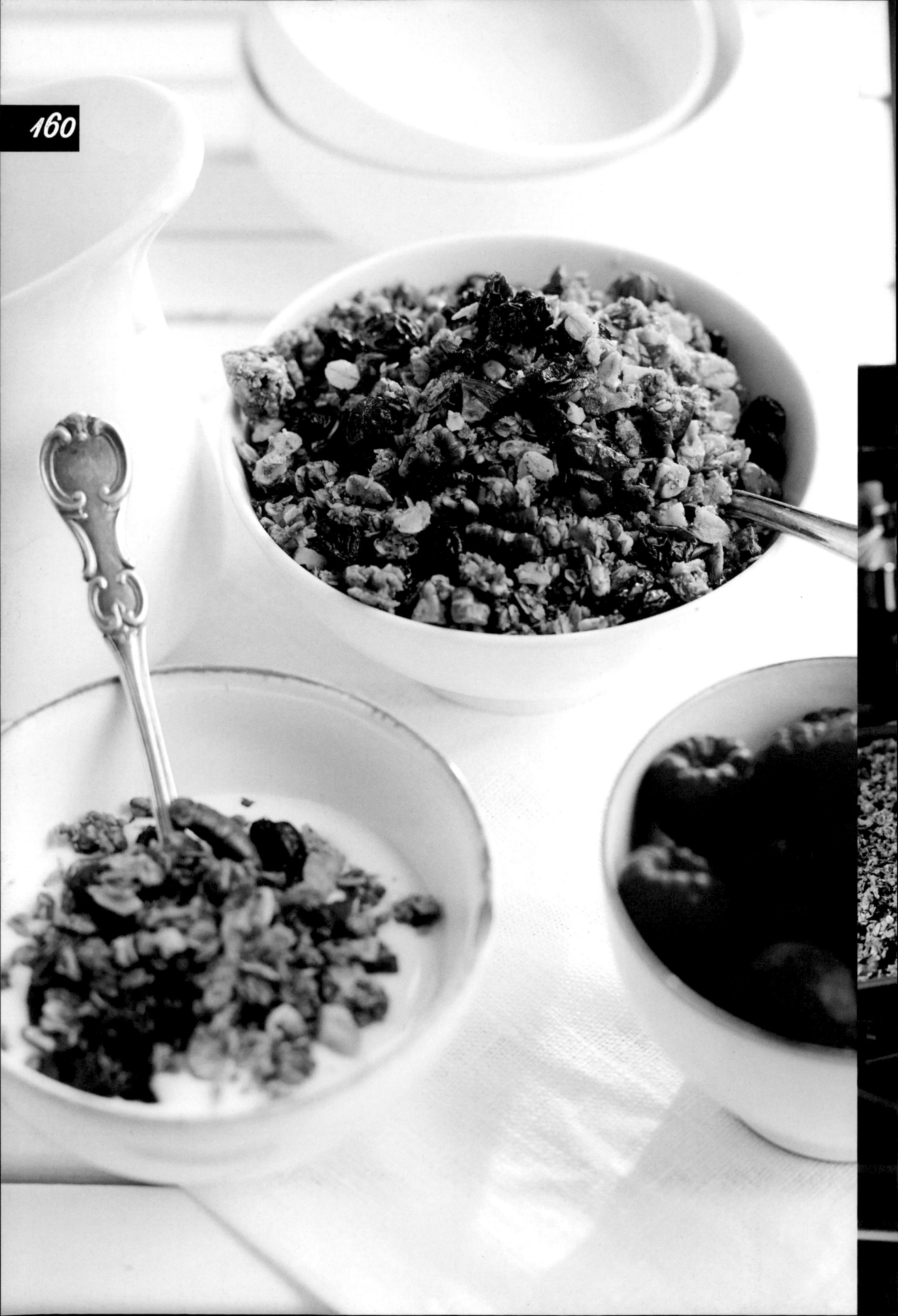

GRANOLA

Cereal and granola are classic breakfast favorites. So why not mix things up and make your own granola?

Approx. 15 portions

½ cup (60 g) sweet almonds
⅓ cup (40 g) pecans
⅓ cup (40 g) walnuts
1⅔ cups (160 g) oatmeal
1⅔ cups (160 g) whole rolled oats
½ cup (40 g) oat bran
⅔ cup (75 g) sunflower seeds
¼ cup (45 g) brown sugar
2½ tbsp (50 g) maple syrup
¼ cup (59 mL (70 g)) honey
⅔ cup (157 mL (150 g)) vegetable oil
¾ tbsp (5 g) ground cinnamon
¼ tbsp (2½ g) vanilla extract
½ tsp (2 g) salt
½ cup (60 g) raisins
½ cup (70 g) dried cranberries

Preheat the oven to 350 degrees Fahrenheit (170 degrees Celsius), convection function. Chop all the nuts and put them in a bowl. Add the oatmeal, whole grain oatmeal, oat bran, and sunflower seeds and mix.

In a saucepan, stir together the brown sugar, maple syrup, honey, oil, cinnamon, vanilla extract, and salt. Bring the mixture to a boil and pour it into the bowl. Mix well and then spread everything out on a baking sheet lined with parchment paper. Roast in the oven for about 23 minutes. Stir the mixture a few times during that period.

Let cool completely and mix in the raisins and cranberries. Keep the dry granola in an airtight jar.

CHEWY OATMEAL COOKIES

Slightly chewy and mildly sweet cookies with a fine, orange flavor. They go well with breakfast, coffee, or a snack.

20 cookies

½ cup (60 g) walnuts
½ cup (60 g) raisins
½ cup (60 g) dried cranberries
1½ cups (120 g) oatmeal
¾ cup (100 g) all-purpose flour
½ tsp (3 g) baking soda
1½ tsp (3 g) ground cinnamon
½ tsp (2 g) salt
½ cup + 1 tsp (120 g) room temperature unsalted butter
¾ cup (125 g) brown sugar
1 (55 g) egg
¼ tbsp (2½ g) vanilla extract
1 orange, grated zest from the whole orange and juice
   from half

Preheat the oven to 350 degrees Fahrenheit (170 degrees Celsius), convection function. Coarsely chop the walnuts and mix with raisins, cranberries, and oatmeal in a bowl. Stir together the flour, baking soda, cinnamon, and salt in a bowl. Beat the butter, vanilla extract, brown sugar, and eggs in another bowl until fluffy. Stir in the flour mixture and work into a dough. Add the nut mixture, orange peel, and juice and mix thoroughly. Wrap the dough in plastic and leave it in the fridge for 20 minutes.

Divide the dough into 20 pieces, roll the pieces into balls, and place them with room between on a baking sheet lined with parchment paper. Flatten the little balls and bake them in the oven for about 10 minutes or until the cookies are golden.

WAFFLES

Waffles don't have to be reserved for waffle day. They can be eaten regularly—regardless of the day.

Approx. 7 waffles

2 (110 g) eggs
1¾ cups (392 mL (425 g)) whole milk
½ tbsp (5 g) vanilla extract
½ cup (118 mL (120 g)) vegetable oil
1⅔ cups (240 g) all-purpose flour
2 tbsp (25 g) sugar
1 tbsp (15 g) baking powder
½ tsp (2 g) salt
Melted butter for brushing the waffles

FOR SERVING
Powdered sugar for dusting
1 ¼ cups (295 mL (300 g)) whipping cream
Fresh strawberries
Maple syrup

Separate the egg yolks and egg whites. Whisk together the milk, oil, vanilla extract, and egg yolks lightly in a bowl. Sift the dry ingredients in a separate bowl. In batches, whisk the dry ingredients into milk mixture and continue whisking until it becomes a smooth batter. Beat the egg whites to a firm meringue and fold into the batter with a spatula.

Cook the waffles for a few minutes or until they turn a nice golden brown color. Brush the waffle iron lightly with butter in between waffles. Dust the waffles with powdered sugar and serve with lightly whipped cream, strawberries, and maple syrup.

BANANA CHOCOLATE CHIP PUDDING

This is what I call a sweet breakfast. Bananas, vanilla, chocolate, cookies, and a little meringue on top. Can you start the day better than this? Extremely good.

PUDDING

Preheat the oven to 325 degrees Fahrenheit (160 degrees Celsius), convection function. Combine the flour and salt in a bowl. Mix the vanilla extract with the milk in a pan. Bring to a boil, stirring occasionally. Whisk in the dry ingredients in batches. Reduce heat, stir in the condensed milk, then egg yolks. Heat the mixture while constantly stirring until it has become a loose cream. Pass the cream through a sieve.

Slice the bananas. Place the digestive cookies in the bottom of each form, then distribute half of the banana slices and chocolate chips on top. Pour in half of the cream and repeat the procedure with another similar layer.

MERINGUE

Beat the egg whites to a firm meringue. Add the sugar in batches and whisk for a further 3-4 minutes. Spread meringue over the puddings and bake in the middle of the oven for about 15 minutes or until the meringue has turned a fine golden brown color. Let cool for 30 minutes and serve.

7 portions of pudding

PUDDING

- ⅓ cup (40 g) all-purpose flour
- 1 pinch of salt
- 1 tsp vanilla extract
- 1⅓ cups (392 mL (400 g)) whole milk
- 1 can (ca 400 g) sweetened condensed milk
- 2 (30 g) egg yolks
- 4 large bananas
- 15 (200 g) graham crackers
- ¼ cup (50 g) dark chocolate chips or chopped dark chocolate

MERINGUE

- 4 (140 g) egg whites
- ¼ cup (50 g) sugar

CINNAMON ROLLS

Personally, I think nothing can beat Swedish cinnamon buns, but the advantage of baking them in a form is that they're more moist and keep longer.

FILLING

Add the almond paste into a bowl (optionally, coarsely grate it first) and mix in the butter in batches. Add sugar and cinnamon and mix thoroughly.

FLOUR DOUGH

Grease the edges of a form 13 × 8.5 inches (32 cm x 22 cm), and the cover bottom with parchment paper. Crumble the yeast in a bowl, preferably a stand mixer. Warm the milk to lukewarm, pour it in the bowl, and dissolve the yeast. Add the remaining ingredients and run for a minute on low speed. Increase speed and run for 6-8 minutes or until the dough feels pliable and has got a nice, shiny finish.

Turn the dough out onto a floured work surface and let it rest 5 minutes. Then roll it out to a disk, 20 x 12 inch (50 × 30 cm). Spread an even layer of filling on top and sprinkle with raisins. Roll into a slightly tight roll from the long side.

Cut the roll in 15 pieces and place the pieces in the pan. Cover with a kitchen towel and let rise until doubled in size. This takes 1 ½–2 hours.

During that time preheat the oven to 400 degrees Fahrenheit (200 degrees Celsius), convection function. Brush the buns with egg, place the pan in the middle of the oven and reduce the heat to 350 degrees Fahrenheit (180 degrees Celsius). Bake for about 25 minutes in the middle of the oven or until the buns are a nice golden brown color. Let the buns cool completely.

GLAZE

Heat the milk and butter in a saucepan until the butter has melted. Add the powdered sugar and vanilla and whisk on low heat until it becomes a rich glaze. Pour the glaze over the rolls and let it solidify.

15 buns

FILLING

7 oz (200 g) almond paste
1 cup + 2 tbsp (250 g) room temperature salted butter
¼ cup (45 g) sugar
2 tbsp (14 g) ground cinnamon
½ cup (80 g) raisins

FLOUR DOUGH

1 oz (25 g) yeast for sweet dough
¾ cup (177 mL (25 g)) whole milk
3 cups (420 g) all-purpose flour
1 (55 g) egg, lightly beaten
½ tsp (2 g) salt
1 tbsp (7 g) ground cardamom
⅓ cup (80 g) butter
½ cup (90 g) sugar
1 whisked egg for brushing

GLAZE

1¾ tbsp (25 mL (25 g)) whole milk
1 tbsp + 1 tsp (20 g) butter
1¼ cups (180 g) powdered sugar
½ tsp (1½ g) vanilla extract

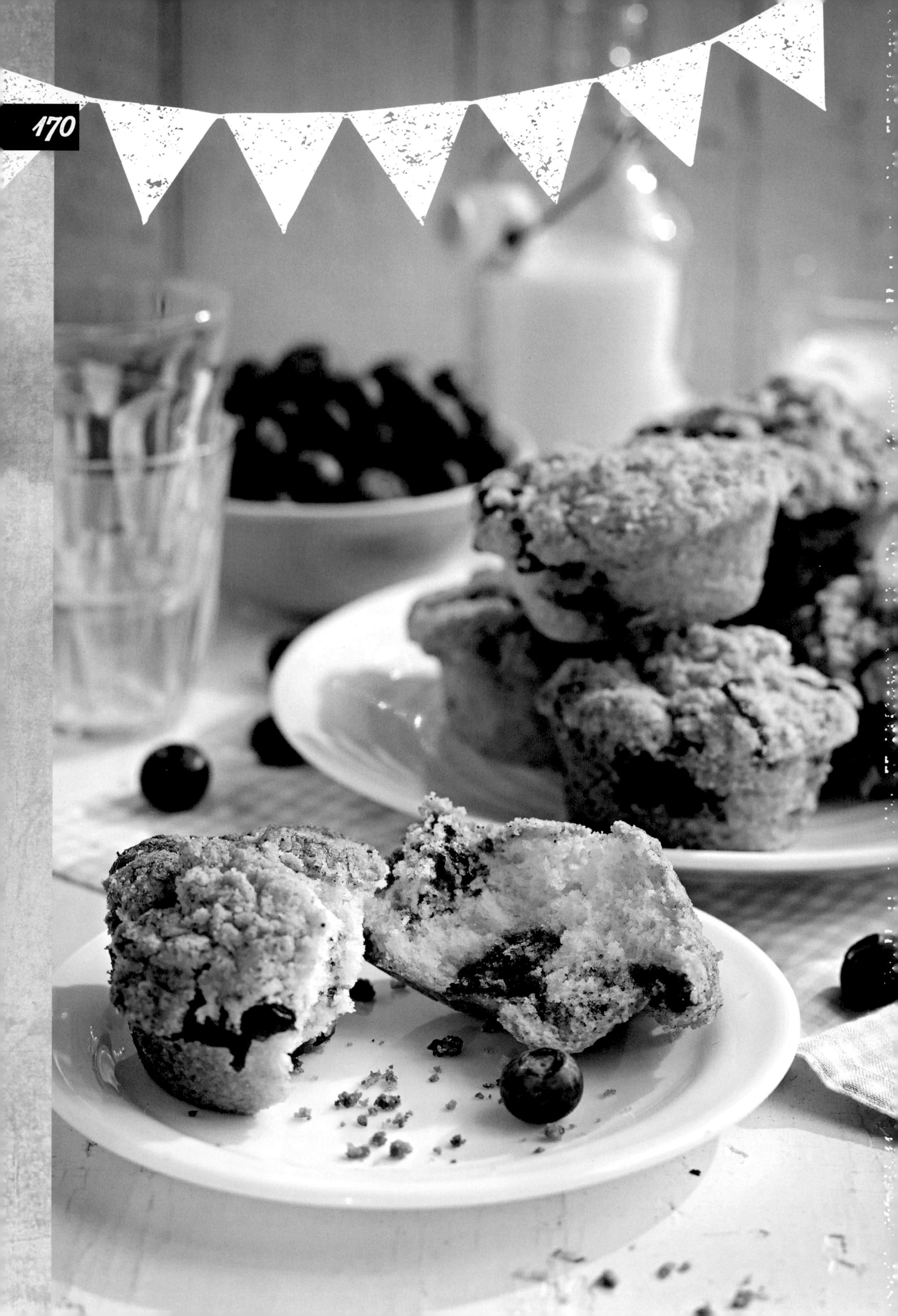

BLUEBERRY MUFFINS

A quick and easy recipe for muffins that taste like blueberry pie. The crumble on top gives them a wonderful crunch. *So* good!

Preheat the oven to 400 degrees Fahrenheit (200 degrees Celsius), convection function. Grease and lightly flour a muffin pan or use doubled-up muffin wrappers placed on a conventional baking tray.

Sift the dry ingredients in a bowl. Lightly whisk together the oil, vanilla extract, egg, and milk in another bowl.

Fold in the dry ingredients with a spatula. Add the blueberries and lemon zest and mix until it becomes a smooth batter. Spread the batter into the molds.

CRUMBLE

Mix all the ingredients in a bowl and pinch together to form a crumble.

Sprinkle the crumbs over the muffins and bake in middle of oven for about 20 minutes. Use a toothpick to make sure the muffins are baked through. Let cool for a few minutes and remove from the form.

10 muffins

1¼ cups (180 g) all-purpose flour
¾ cup (160 g) sugar
2 tsp (9 g) baking powder
½ tsp (3 g) salt
¼ tbsp (2½ g) vanilla extract
½ cup (118 mL (85 g)) vegetable oil
1 (55 g) egg
⅓ cup (79 mL (75 g)) whole milk
⅔ cup (150 g) fresh blueberries
Grated zest from one lemon

CRUMBLE

½ cup (85 g) sugar
⅓ cup (40 g) all-purpose flour
¼ cup (50 g) room temperature salted butter
1½ tsp (3 g) ground cinnamon

INDEX

THANKS

A big thank you with all my heart to all the family members and friends who have been involved and supported me in this project. Without you, this dream could not have come true. An extra big thanks to photographer Wolfgang Kleinschmidt for a fantastic and successful cooperation – both on location in LA and in the studio. A warm thank you to GANT and Ljung for loaning me the clothes. Also, warm thanks to Niko Järvikari for styling my clothes.

First published in 2013 as *United States of Cakes* by Roy Fares,
Bonnier Fakta, Sweden
Photography by Wolfgang Kleinschmidt
Props by Tove Nilsson
Graphic Design by Elina Grandin
Skyhorse edition edited by Amy Li

Skyhorse Publishing books may be purchased in bulk at special
discounts for sales promotion, corporate gifts, fund-raising, or
educational purposes. Special editions can also be created to
specifications. For details, contact the Special Sales Department,
Skyhorse Publishing, 307 West 36th Street, 11th Floor, New York, NY
10018 or info@skyhorsepublishing.com.

Skyhorse® and Skyhorse Publishing® are registered trademarks of
Skyhorse Publishing, Inc.®, a Delaware corporation.
www.skyhorsepublishing.com

10 9 8 7 6 5 4 3 2 1

Library of Congress Cataloging-in-Publication Data
is available on file.

Cover design by Daniel Brount

Print ISBN: 978-1-5107-6489-7
eBook ISBN: 978-1-63450-112-5

Printed in China